you know you're in
texas when...

Some Other Books in the Series

You Know You're In Series

you know you're in
texas when...

101 quintessential places, people, events,
customs, lingo, and eats of the lone star state

Donna Ingham

INSIDERS' GUIDE®

GUILFORD, CONNECTICUT
AN IMPRINT OF THE GLOBE PEQUOT PRESS

INSIDERS' GUIDE®

Text design by Linda R. Loiewski
Illustrations by Sue Mattero

Library of Congress Cataloging-in-Publication Data
Ingham, Donna.
    You know you're in Texas when— : 101 quintessential places, people, events, customs, lingo, and eats of the Lone Star State / Donna Ingham. — 1st ed.
      p. cm. — (You know you're in series)
  Includes index.
  ISBN-13: 978-0-7627-3811-3
  ISBN-10: 0-7627-3811-1
  1. Texas—Miscellanea. 2. Texas—Description and travel—Miscellanea. I. Title.
  F386.6.I55 2006
  976.4—dc22

                                                              2006020811

Manufactured in the United States of America
First Edition/First Printing

To Jerry and Christopher, again and always

about the author

Donna Ingham is a Texan born and bred and has heard Texas stories all her life. Now she writes them and tells them for fun and profit. A former college English professor, she currently tours the country as a professional storyteller—except for the times she holes up in her study to write a book like *Tales with a Texas Twist* (Globe Pequot, 2005) or this one. Ingham lives in Spicewood with her husband, Jerry.

to the reader

The trouble with writing a book about Texas is that everyone already has very definite notions about Texas, even people who have never lived in the Lone Star State—maybe *especially* people who have never lived in the Lone Star State.

Say the word *Texas,* and it's like the start of a rapid-fire word-association game. I say Texas: You say cowboys. I say Texas: You say oil wells. Texas: rattlesnakes. Texas: big hair. Texas: barbecue. Texas: rodeos. Texas: the Alamo. Texas: longhorns. Well, you get the idea.

Some of the entries in this book were clearly dictated by readers' expectations, and legitimately so. All those things mentioned above are part of Texas's image—both the mythic one and the real one—and must be included. But, oh, there's so much more.

Texas is bluebonnets in the spring, blue northers in the winter, and Blue Bell ice cream any time. Texas is Aggie jokes, Big Tex, and the Cadillac Ranch. Texas is Willie Nelson, Lance Armstrong, and LBJ. Texas is Juneteenth, the Kerrville Folk Festival, and a trip to San Antonio's River Walk.

Of course, Texans have a reputation for being overly proud of their state, but Texas does have a number of legitimate claims to having the biggest, the tallest, the longest, the most, the first, and the only. Some of those are included in this book as well.

But mostly Texans try to live up to the state motto: friendship. They're quick to say "Y'all come and sit a spell. Have some barbecue or Tex-Mex, and let's swap some tall tales or listen to some Western swing." They may offer you a Lone Star—the beer, not the flag—or a cold Dr Pepper. They'll talk about the weather, football, and the price of pickups.

And they'll make you feel welcome in this diverse, quirky, uniquely shaped state that once was its own country. That's when you'll know you're really in Texas.

you know you're in
texas when...
...the joke's on A&M

Why do Aggies hate M&Ms?
They're too hard to peel.

Did you hear about the Aggie who asked what time Midnight Yell Practice began?

How many Aggies does it take to screw in a lightbulb?
One, but he gets three hours' credit.

These are typical of the jokes that have targeted the Aggie mascot of Texas A&M University for years. No one knows who started telling the jokes or when, but the why of the matter likely has everything to do with college rivalries.

Especially for A&M's athletic conference rivals, telling Aggie jokes has long been a fall ritual to prepare for big games. A charter member of the Southwest Conference until its dissolution in 1996, the Aggies now compete in the Big 12 Conference, and A&M's major rival is the University of Texas.

Their annual football game is billed as the Lone Star Showdown. As one might suspect, students and alumni from the University of Texas are particularly prone to poke fun at the Aggies by suggesting they're not very bright.

Actually, Texas A&M is the oldest and one of the most respected academic institutions in the state. Founded in 1876 as an

Aggie Jokes:

College rivalries have spawned the put-downs, but Aggies get some laughs with clever quips of their own.

An Aggie and a Longhorn walk into a bar . . .

agricultural and mechanical college, it is one of the top 10 universities attracting National Merit Scholars in the United States. Its academic programs—most notably those in engineering, architecture, and business—consistently rank high in national surveys. And the College Station campus is one of the largest in the nation.

The Aggies have figured out a way to turn the tables on their would-be detractors by using jokes themselves to market the school. For example . . .

What do you call an Aggie after graduation?
Boss.

Three major airlines are headquartered in Texas: Continental is in Houston, American in Fort Worth, and Southwest in Dallas. It's the last two that got entangled in what we might call the airport wars.

Dallas and Fort Worth have always had a bit of a rivalry going; it extended to travel when they couldn't agree to partner up on a joint airport. Actually, Dallas was willing as early as 1927, but Fort Worth wasn't. So Fort Worth built Meacham Field that same year, and Dallas bought Love Field from the military in 1928 and transformed it into a municipal airport.

By the 1960s—after both cities had sought federal funding for their respective airports—the Civil Aeronautics Board got into the mix. The CAB ordered Dallas and Fort Worth to find a suitable site and build a regional airport.

The result was what is now Dallas/Fort Worth International Airport, which officially opened in 1974. Its first commercial flight was American Airlines flight 341. By 1978 American had moved its corporate headquarters from New York to Fort Worth and become the major presence at DFW. It still is.

Meanwhile, in 1971 an upstart airline called Southwest was founded in Dallas and headquartered at Love Field. By the time DFW opened, Southwest was per-fectly happy where it was and didn't want to move. Reenter the feds. To help ensure DFW's success, Congressman Jim Wright of Fort Worth helped pass a compromise law that restricted passenger air traffic out of Love Field.

The Wright Amendment dictated that Southwest could fly passengers from its Love Field terminal only to locations within Texas and four neighboring states: Louisiana, Arkansas, Oklahoma, and New Mexico. Later, four more states were added. Southwest adapted and prospered.

DFW prospered, too. It is the largest and busiest airport in the state. American Airlines operates more than 80 percent of its passenger traffic.

Kind of makes you wonder what all the fuss is about, doesn't it?

Airlines:

Of the three major airlines headquartered in Texas, American and Southwest are most affected by the Wright Amendment.

Texas general Sam Houston once suggested that it would be better to "blow up the Alamo and abandon the place." Thankfully for Texas tourism, he was overruled.

Houston's comment came just before the famous battle between Texan and Mexican forces on March 6, 1836. We all know how *that* turned out. But not everyone knows that the Alamo was around for more than a century before that defining moment in history.

It was built in 1718 as San Antonio de Valero Mission, a way station between the Rio Grande and the Spanish missions in East Texas. After three moves from its original location west of San Pedro Creek, the mission was placed at its current site in 1724. The chapel featured on postcards today was constructed during the 1750s.

Whence the name *Alamo?* Historians aren't sure whether it came from a nearby grove of cottonwoods (*álamo* in Spanish) or from the company of soldiers housed at the mission in 1803 (they were from Álamo de Parras in Mexico). The real mystery, however, is how the Alamo survived at all.

First came Houston's proposal. Then Mexican general Antonio López de Santa Anna followed suit and ordered the Alamo destroyed after his victory there. Legend has it that ghostly sentries held the demolition details at bay. Unfortunately, the living

The Alamo:

Even though Texans lost their battle there, it is the most visited historic site in the state.

weren't so conscientious. By the end of the 19th century, the mission-turned-fortress had fallen into serious disrepair.

Enter Clara Driscoll, daughter of a multimillionaire, granddaughter of two veterans of the Texas Revolution, and a young woman committed to the idea of historic preservation. From 1903 to 1905 she worked with the Daughters of the Republic of Texas to acquire and preserve the Alamo, paying most of the purchase price herself. Driscoll quickly became known as the "Savior of the Alamo."

Now celebrated as a shrine of Texas independence from Mexico, the Alamo is open to the public year-round. For more information, visit www.thealamo.org.

you know you're in
texas when...
... not only chickens cross the road

Any armadillo in Texas can tell you that crossing a highway is a health hazard. Armadillos have few natural enemies, but automobiles are certainly among their chief agents of mortality.

A fairly recent addition to Texas fauna, armadillos ambled up from Central and South America by way of Mexico in the 19th century. About the size of a small dog or a large cat, they are distinctive because of their armorlike shell, which is actually two shields—one over the shoulders, one over the rump—with nine bands in the middle. (The Texas species is therefore called the "nine-banded armadillo.")

Partial to all kinds of bugs, armadillos have a keen sense of smell and can sniff out a tasty meal 6 inches underground. They like water but can't swim worth a hoot, thanks to that heavy shell. But they manage. If a stream is not too wide, an armadillo will simply enter on one side, walk across the bottom (under water), and emerge on the other side. Faced with a wider expanse, the armadillo will ingest air, inflating itself and increasing its buoyancy enough to swim across.

Armadillos have been giving up their shells for the Texas souvenir trade since the late 19th century, when the armadillo-shell basket was invented. The shells have also been fashioned into lamps and other curios.

Armadillo:

The armadillo was designated the state small mammal by the 74th Legislature in 1995.

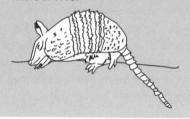

During the Great Depression many East Texans stocked their larders with what they called "Hoover hogs," a reference to the armadillo's porklike taste (although some insisted that they really taste like chicken) and to President Herbert Hoover, whom they considered responsible for the depression.

In the 1970s armadillo racing became a popular amusement. Several organizations from San Angelo and elsewhere in the state began promoting the races—not just in Texas but throughout the United States, in Canada, and even in Europe.

Handling armadillos can be a little risky, however, as they are the only mammal other than humans known to carry Hansen's disease, or leprosy. For this reason, it is illegal to sell a live armadillo in the state of Texas.

Bikers of the pedaling kind take to the hills in Texas. Many of them take their inspiration from Lance Armstrong, Tour de France champion for a record seven consecutive times.

From 1999 to 2005 he proved himself to be the best in the world in the most grueling contest devised for the sport of cycling. That's an accomplishment difficult enough for any athlete, but in Armstrong's case, it's truly amazing.

This lanky Texas boy, who grew up in the Dallas suburb of Plano (and now lives in Austin), tried first to play football, as most boys do in this football-crazed state. But he wasn't coordinated enough to be successful. So he took up distance running and joined the swim club. Before Armstrong reached high school, he had competed in triathlons. Then came the bike and the bike races, and he'd found his sport.

Armstrong seemed to be reaching his potential in 1996, when his world ranking jumped to number one. Then he was diagnosed with stage 3 testicular cancer. Doctors said he had, at best, a 50–50 chance of surviving, much less riding his bicycle again—especially after the cancer metastasized and spread to his lungs and brain.

Yet less than a year after surgery and aggressive chemotherapy, he began training again—and by 1998 he was back in competition. Armstrong's first Tour de France win in 1999 marked his real comeback and began a legendary string of victories that climaxed with his seventh win in 2005 and his retirement at age 33.

In 1997 he formed the Lance Armstrong Foundation to raise cancer awareness and give aid and support to those in need. He also launched his annual fund-raising Ride for the Roses, held in Austin. But it may be a simple yellow rubber wristband that will top all fund-raising efforts.

With only the motto *livestrong* stamped into it, the $1.00 bracelet has become a fashion statement all over the world. It has raised about $50 million to date and is still in high demand. For more information, visit www.lancearmstrong.com and www.livestrong.org.

Armstrong, Lance:

The seven-time Tour de France winner trained in the Texas Hill Country and continues to raise millions for cancer awareness.

It's not uncommon for Texas women to have and use double names, but few have parlayed their names into worldwide recognition quite like Mary Kay. Mary Kay Ash, that is. She launched Mary Kay Cosmetics in 1963, investing her life savings of $5,000 and starting with a sales force of 11 people.

Born Mary Kathlyn Wagner in Houston in 1915, Ash had learned firsthand about direct sales by peddling psychology books door-to-door, working part-time for Stanley Home Products, and becoming a national training director for World Gift Company. When one of her male colleagues at the latter company got promoted over her—at twice her salary—Ash quit. A month later, she created her own company.

Her business plan was simple: Find a good product, follow the Golden Rule, and live by the motto "God first, family second, career third." Ash bought a formula for a skin-care cream developed by an Arkansas tanner and promoted it as a beauty product. She recruited friends and her two sons to help sell "Beauty by Mary Kay."

From the outset she provided motivation and offered incentives. She often pointed out, "Aerodynamically, the bumblebee shouldn't be able to fly, but the bumblebee doesn't know that, so it goes on flying anyway." As one who had experienced gender discrimination in the workplace, she was determined to encourage the women who worked for her to fly right to the top.

Her company therefore rewards its top salespeople with a symbolic diamond bumblebee pin. But the best-known incentive is the pink Cadillac awarded to those who become national sales directors. In fact, if any company can be said to own the color pink, it may be Mary Kay Cosmetics; its compacts and makeup boxes are also pink.

When Ash died in 2001, the company's sales force had grown to more than 750,000 in 37 countries, and wholesale revenue had reached $1.3 billion.

Ash, Mary Kay:

This business phenom parlayed a small direct-sales company into the largest direct seller of skin care and color cosmetics in the United States.

you know you're in
texas when...
...cemeteries host extraterrestrials

The town that almost wasn't, according to its local history, claims to have buried an alien that really was.

Legend has it that a spaceship crashed into a windmill near Aurora, north of Fort Worth, in 1897 and that a tiny pilot was found among the wreckage. According to one version, the alien was still alive but the town doctor was unable to save him.

So, it's said, the extraterrestrial visitor was buried in the Aurora Cemetery. There is even photographic evidence of a headstone long since missing and presumed stolen. The *Dallas Morning News* reported the amazing event in its April 19, 1897, issue, noting that the pilot of the airship was "not an inhabitant of this world."

Renewed interest in the site in the 1970s grew out of articles carried by United Press International and the Associated Press. A film version of the story, *Aurora Encounter*, premiered in 1986 and starred Jack Elam.

Visitors interested in UFOs came to Aurora. One group wanted to exhume the pilot's remains. By this time, however, no one was sure where the alleged grave was since there was no stone to mark it. The cemetery board nixed the request, saying that it didn't want searchers digging up the whole place.

Aurora Cemetery:

With graves dating from as early as the 1860s, its most intriguing inhabitant may be an alien crash victim.

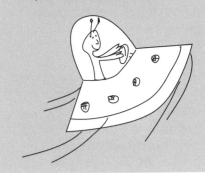

Dismissed as a hoax by most, the story persists, and the cemetery continues to draw the curious. The historical marker at the cemetery labels as legend the report "that a spaceship crashed nearby in 1897 and the pilot, killed in the crash, was buried here." But some folks still want to believe.

you know you're in
texas when...
...you want your meat smoked

Looking for the best barbecue in Texas? Check out those small-town joints with a smoky patina on the walls and a big pit (or several) on the premises. From there on it's a matter of taste. Sauce, rub, or neither? Mesquite, oak, or hickory? Beef, pork, or chicken? There's even dispute about the spelling of the word: *barbecue, barbeque, bar-b-que, BBQ*.

Central Texas has many of the top-rated barbecue eateries in the state, at least according to *Texas Monthly* magazine's periodic listing. Try Kreutz Market in Lockhart, Louie Mueller Barbeque in Taylor, Cooper's Old Time Pit Bar-B-Que in Llano, and the Salt Lick in Driftwood. Of course, there are thousands of others—really—all over the state, so choosing the absolute best is an exercise in futility.

What most Texas barbecue connoisseurs do agree on, however, is that the preferred cut of meat is beef brisket—and that it should be smoked in a pit until it is tender enough to pull apart with your fingers. The usual sides include cheap white sandwich bread, pinto beans, potato salad, and cole slaw. The most authentic restaurants serve everything on sheets of white butcher paper or, at best, plastic plates. You get a roll of paper towels for clean-up. We're talking no frills here.

It's possible to order pork ribs or chops or sausage or chicken or even mutton or goat, but clearly what defines Texas barbecue is beef. And wood smoke. And a general aversion to sauce. Sauce may be available, but it's likely to be served on the side, and it tends to be thin, tart, and vinegary, with a tomato and chili powder base.

My advice: Arrive at your chosen barbecue joint early, when the meat is just coming off the pit. Most places run out of it long before closing time, so you might miss out on the brisket if you're late.

Barbecue:

Sure, you can get ribs and chicken and sausage, but for a real taste of Texas, you've got to order brisket.

you know you're in
texas when...
...you look beyond the belfry

"Keep Austin Weird." The city's unofficial slogan may account for one of its prime summertime leisure activities: bat-watching along the Congress Avenue bridge downtown.

Renovations to the bridge over Town Lake in 1980 created narrow but deep openings on its underside that turned out to be perfect accommodations for Mexican free-tailed bats. Estimates range from 750,000 up to 1.5 million of the winged mammals at the peak of bat-watching season (which runs March to October), making this urban bat colony the largest in North America.

The best bat views are in August, when bat pups join their mothers in evening flights and emerge from under the bridge in a dark cloud that can swirl up and away for as long as 45 minutes. Watchers line up on the sidewalks along the bridge or seek out public viewing areas provided by nearby businesses.

Not as accessible, but certainly impressive, is Bracken Cave, near San Antonio, which has an even larger colony of Mexican free-tailed bats. (It qualifies as the largest aggregation of warm-blooded animals on earth.) Millions of the bats fly out to hunt each evening and consume some 200 tons of flying insects, making them beneficial to farmers whose corn and cotton crops are thus less threatened by the pests.

Bats:

When they're in residence beneath a downtown bridge in Austin, their evening flights draw big crowds of spectators.

All told, Texas is home to 32 of the 45 bat species in the United States, but none has become as popular or as plentiful as the Mexican free-tailed variety, now the official state flying mammal.

If ships could talk, what stories they could tell. That's especially true of the USS *Texas*, better known as Battleship *Texas*. Commissioned in 1914, it is now the lone survivor of its dreadnought class.

Donated to the state by the U.S. Navy in 1948, the *Texas* became the first battleship memorial museum in the United States. It is permanently moored in the Houston Ship Channel on Buffalo Bayou at the San Jacinto Battleground.

Among other firsts, in 1916 the *Texas* became the first U.S. battleship to mount antiaircraft guns and in 1919 the first to launch an aircraft. In 1939 it received the first commercial radar in the U.S. Navy. During her military career, the *Texas* served in both the Atlantic and Pacific Oceans and saw battle at Normandy, Iwo Jima, and Okinawa. At the end of World War I, she escorted the German Fleet en route to its surrender anchorage, and during World War II she put Texan Walter Cronkite ashore to begin his career as a war correspondent.

In spite of her long and illustrious history, the *Texas* might not have survived without private donations and the efforts of state residents and businesses. Even school-age children gave their pennies to save the *Texas*. The ship underwent dry dock overhaul from 1988 to 1990. Instead of battle-

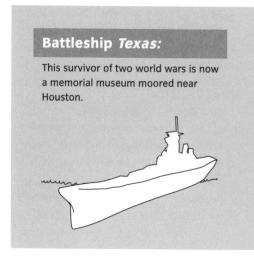

Battleship *Texas:*

This survivor of two world wars is now a memorial museum moored near Houston.

ship gray, she was painted the same blue camouflage she wore during service in the Pacific in 1945.

These days visitors can experience history firsthand as they tour the storied ship, now commissioned as the flagship of the Texas Navy.

you know you're in
texas when...
...the open spaces are extra wide

If you're looking for a landscape rugged and largely unpopulated to the point of downright isolation, then drive on down to Big Bend Country. That is truly a place where you can get away from it all.

Oh, there are pockets of civilization, to be sure, eager innkeepers and restaurant owners ready to feed you and put you up for the night. But for the most part, the area looks like a backdrop for a western movie, with its spectacular mountain and desert scenery.

Big Bend Country lies south of the Davis Mountains and gets its name from its location in a great southward swing of the Rio Grande, which borders it on three sides. It has its own mountains, the Chisos, and three noteworthy canyons along the Rio Grande: Santa Elena, Mariscal, and Boquillas. The rest is Chihuahuan desert.

The southern part of the region along the Rio Grande is home to Big Bend National Park (www.nps.gov/bibe/)—all 801,000 acres of it. It was the first national park in Texas, established in 1944. From the start the National Park Service recognized the landscape as "decidedly the outstanding scenic area in Texas." To this day the NPS proposes only basic improvements, thus allowing the park's natural zones to "remain largely unaltered by human activity."

If your idea of a good time is being surrounded by lots of human activity and shopping at the mall, Big Bend is not for you. If, on the other hand, you're into hiking, birding, and float trips, come on down. Or you can simply plan to take a leisurely drive between Marathon and Alpine.

Just in case the expanse of the national park is not enough for you, there's always Big Bend Ranch State Park (www.tpwd .state.tx.us), with almost 300,000 acres extending along the Rio Grande from southeast of Presidio to near Lajitas.

Needless to say, a visit to Big Bend is more than a day trip.

Big Bend:

The bend is in the Rio Grande, but the country it encompasses on three sides is one of the most ruggedly beautiful areas in Texas.

you know you're in
texas when...
...hairdos are defining features

What "big" is bigger in Texas than "big hair"? Sometime in the 1960s it started—the backcombing or teasing or ratting, as it was variously known, that created a larger-than-life bouffant hairstyle. The 'do was sprayed to helmet hardness so that it was capable of withstanding even the strongest winds (that can be very important in some parts of Texas).

Prior to the backcombing, of course, came the "setting" of the hair on giant rollers the size of frozen juice cans. Do-it-yourselfers who couldn't afford the time or money to go to the beauty shop figured out ingenious ways to arrange their bed pillows so that they could actually sleep with the rollers in place and let their hair dry overnight.

The hairstyle took root when Lady Bird Johnson was First Lady but reached its peak, so to speak, in the 1970s when the world consulted the TV show *Dallas* to see what Texas women looked like. They looked like they had big hair. Then Corpus Christi native Farrah Fawcett wore a kind of winged version of big hair on *Charlie's Angels*. It was definitely a fashion statement.

Even former Texas governor Ann Richards was described as having big hair. Keeping her sense of humor about the whole thing,

she declared an official Texas Big Hair Day in 1993.

Some—especially those ladies who championed the style—saw big hair as an emblem of rich, powerful, glamorous women. Others thought it was tacky and, well, over the top.

You can still see big hair in Texas, but a lot of it is tinted blue these days.

Big Hair:

When women have to duck while walking under the ceiling fan, you know they've been backcombing again.

There's at least one sure 'nough big old boy at the State Fair of Texas in Dallas. No 10-gallon hat for this 52-foot-tall cowboy, no sir. His is a 75-gallon Stetson to go with his size 70 boots and his quintuple-extra-large jeans.

His name is Big Tex, and he's been the official symbol of the state fair since 1952. When he celebrated his 50th birthday in 2002, the AARP gave him a lifetime membership card.

But how he got to Dallas is kind of an interesting story. You see, he started out as Santa Claus. That's right. Chamber of commerce members in the little town of Kerens, Texas, 75 miles south of Dallas, built what they claimed was the world's largest Santa Claus out of iron-pipe drill casing and papier-mâché. They used 7-foot lengths of unraveled rope for his beard.

Santa drew some crowds his inaugural year, 1949. But the novelty soon wore off, and town leaders sold his components to the state fair in 1951 for $750.

After a preliminary makeover, he emerged 3 feet taller as a cowboy with a crooked nose and what was described as a "lascivious wink." More cosmetic surgery straightened his nose and got rid of the wink so that he looked more like his designer, Jack Bridges, with a little bit of the visage of a

Big Tex:

This 52-foot-tall cowboy is the undisputed "world's tallest Texan."

local rancher and of Will Rogers thrown in for good measure.

The tall, strong, silent type his first year, Big Tex got his voice in 1953 and began welcoming fairgoers with his slow Texas drawl. After being animated as a bionic man, he began giving his friendly wave in 1997 and turning his head in 2000. An extreme makeover in 1997 replaced his original materials so that he now has a fiberglass head with a jaw that moves and a cagelike skeleton consisting of 4,200 feet of steel rods that weigh three tons.

For more information about Big Tex and the State Fair of Texas, call (214) 565–9931 or visit www.bigtex.com.

you know you're in
texas when...
... a timer comes with dinner

Anyone looking for a really big steak must head to Amarillo and the Big Texan Steak Ranch on Interstate 40.

The story is that owner Bob Lee came to Amarillo in the late 1950s and couldn't find a big steak dinner served in an authentic Western setting. Within a year he opened his own cowboy steak house on old Route 66 (later moved to its current location).

Because his aim was to serve the largest steak in Texas, Lee claims that he found a cowboy with the biggest appetite he'd ever seen and fed the cowboy steak until he was full. Then Lee calculated the intake and figured that the cowboy had consumed 72 ounces of beef, roughly equivalent to a four-and-a-half-pound roast. "That's how big I knew my biggest steak had to be," Lee said.

The 72-ounce steak dinner is advertised as free—if you can eat it and all the sides in under an hour. To date, thousands have tried it, and many have succeeded. One fellow with a strong cutting hand and generous helpings of A-1 steak sauce polished off the meal in less than 10 minutes. Women compete, too; on average, two women each year leave the table victorious.

The popularity and success of the promotion has earned it the National Restaurant Association's MVP (most valuable promo-

Big Texan Steak Ranch:

This Amarillo restaurant is the home of the 72-ounce steak dinner—free if you can eat it all in under an hour.

tion) award and garnered attention for the Big Texan in publications and on television shows nationwide.

The restaurant compound has grown to include a gift shop, a bar, a shooting gallery, banquet rooms, and the Big Texan Motel, complete with its own Texas-shaped swimming pool. In 2004 the 20-stall Horse Hotel was added behind the main motel building. See www.bigtexan.com for more information.

Quick: Name a critter associated with Texas. Did you say golden-cheeked warbler? Well, maybe you should have. Longhorns and armadillos may dominate the state's bumper stickers, but it's the birds that are drawing record numbers of visitors.

Bird-watchers, or birders as they prefer to be called these days, are themselves flocking to Texas to add new sightings to their lists. There are almost 600 bird species in Texas, more than any other state or province in North America.

Some of these winged creatures can be seen nowhere else in the United States. Green jays, Altamira orioles, and chachalacas make their home in the Rio Grande Valley, for example. Endangered golden-cheeked warblers breed entirely within the boundaries of the state and fledge from nests in the Hill Country of central Texas. The red-cockaded woodpecker—which is on the endangered species list—is a local resident in the piney woods of east Texas.

The most amazing Texas bird story may be the one about the whooping crane. The tallest of all North American birds, the whooping crane was facing extinction in 1941 when its numbers were down to 15 birds in one flock wintering at what was then the Aransas Migratory Waterfowl Refuge in south Texas.

Texans took note—as did Canadians, given that whoopers nest in northern Canada, roughly 2,400 miles away. And so began "a love affair of two nations with a great white bird."

Better protection of habitat and a program to raise some of the birds in captivity have increased the numbers of whooping cranes that make it back to winter in Texas each year. They land in what is now Aransas National Wildlife Refuge (361–286–3559) on a broad peninsula about 12 miles across Aransas Bay northeast of Rockport. Although they are still on the endangered list, the whoopers number more than 100 now.

The best time to see them and other wildlife along the Texas Coastal Birding Trail is from November through March, when the greatest numbers of species are at the refuge.

Birding:

Folks come from around the world to Texas in hopes of glimpsing some of the birds rarely, if ever, seen in other parts of the country.

In the world of politics, ties between Washington and Texas apparently all "hinge on a one-quart tub."

At least, that's what the Texas congressional delegation says. In 2005 they mounted a bipartisan effort to pass TEXWAFTA, the Texas–Washington Free Trade Agreement. Their goal: to get Blue Bell ice cream delivered to our nation's capital, of course.

That's how desperate some Texans get when they move somewhere that Blue Bell products aren't sold. Because the company delivers all its own ice cream and doesn't make a run to D.C., however, the congressmen's only recourse is to follow the lead of one resident at 1600 Pennsylvania Avenue and have several half gallons shipped overnight, costly though that might be.

First called the Brenham Creamery Company, "the little creamery in Brenham," as it characterizes itself, opened its doors in 1907. At first it made only butter, but by 1911 it was cranking out a gallon or two of ice cream per day.

The horse and wagon used for early deliveries were traded for a horseless carriage in the late 1920s. By 1930 the name was changed to Blue Bell Creameries, after a wildflower that grew in the area, and by 1936 the company had its first refrigerated delivery truck and its first continuous ice cream freezer.

Although Blue Bell produces more than 20 flavors year-round and another 20 or more flavors seasonally, its best seller is still Homemade Vanilla, introduced in 1969. In fact, it is the best-selling single flavor of ice cream in the United States.

It's a good thing that Brenham is right in the middle of Texas dairy country. It takes between 40,000 and 50,000 cows to produce the milk used on a daily basis to make Blue Bell ice cream.

The company's advertising slogan is "We eat all we can and sell the rest." Blue Bell sells enough to be the number one ice cream in Texas and third best seller nationwide. For information about tours, call (800) 327–8135 or visit www.bluebell.com.

Blue Bell Ice Cream:

Of all its flavors, Homemade Vanilla is still the favorite.

There is little question that cowboy boots and jeans are among the most recognized fashion contributions to the world. And nowhere is their popularity more noticeable than in Texas.

Western wear in general evolved in response to the environment in which real cowboys and cowgirls worked and was adapted from items worn by Mexican vaqueros. The cowboy boot's high top, for example, protected the lower legs. Its pointed toe helped guide the foot into a saddle stirrup, and the high heel kept the foot from slipping all the way through the stirrup while the cowboy was working.

Jeans were designed to be heavy enough to protect the legs and snug enough to prevent the pant legs from snagging on brush, corral equipment, and other hazards.

What was once merely functional has, over the years, become fashionable, however, and a great many people who have never been near a horse opt for boots and/or jeans as daily wear. Among Texas men, it is not at all uncommon to see lawyers and bankers wearing well-shined boots with their three-piece suits. For a typical Texas ball, their ensemble consists of a traditional tuxedo jacket, shirt, tie, starched and creased western jeans, black boots, and the biggest belt buckle they can find.

Boots and Jeans:

In Texas we still see how the West was worn.

Texas women also don fashion jeans to wear with high heels, fancy blouses and jackets, and expensive jewelry (silver and turquoise are popular) for high-falutin' occasions. And they're likely to pair casual jeans with boots or half-boots of their own. Denim stitched up into any kind of garment, as a matter of fact, is a mainstay in almost any Texan's wardrobe.

Among the historically well-known Texas boot-making companies are Justin, Nocona, and Tony Lama. To see a colorful display of Justin boots, visit the John Justin Trail of Fame in the Texas Cowboy Hall of Fame in Fort Worth (www.texascowboy halloffame.com).

Gail Borden Jr. was born in New York in 1801 but kept moving south and west looking for a better climate. He arrived in Texas at Galveston Island on Christmas Eve in 1829 and began accomplishing an impressive list of achievements.

A man of many talents and interests, he first tried farming but soon succeeded his brother as surveyor for Stephen F. Austin's colony in Texas. By 1835 Borden had founded a newspaper and prepared the first topographical map of Texas. He helped design and develop the city of Galveston.

By the mid-1840s Borden had become an inventor. Early on he devised a "locomotive bathhouse" for Galveston women who wished to bathe in the Gulf of Mexico. In 1849 he concocted a meat biscuit from dehydrated meat and flour and moved back to New York to help market it. It was not a big seller—yet Borden's fascination with methods for food preservation would eventually bring him fame and fortune.

More specifically, he turned his attention to condensing milk in a vacuum. He obtained American and British patents in 1856, but his first two factories back East failed. The third succeeded, perhaps because the Civil War brought an increased demand for Borden's condensed milk. Borden was later

Borden, Gail:

He surveyed Stephen F. Austin's colony, prepared the first topographic map of Texas, and designed Galveston, but he's most remembered for one invention: condensed milk.

fond of saying, "I tried and failed. I tried again and again and succeeded."

For the last few years of his life, Borden continued to winter in Texas because of its milder climate, but after his death his body was shipped back to New York for burial. The only reminders of Borden's remarkable tenure in the Lone Star State are the small west Texas town of Gail (named in his honor) and its county, Borden.

The last frontier in the Lone Star State is the Texas–Mexico border, *la frontera*. Following the Rio Grande from El Paso to Brownsville, the borderland reveals a unique blend of the two countries' cultures.

The food is tasty Tex-Mex, the music is conjunto, and borderlanders mingle English and Spanish words in the same sentence. Texans and Mexicans borrow from and contribute to each other's way of life so that the result is a distinct border culture—one that differs considerably from what is found in the heartland of either area.

Part of visiting the Texas border is crossing over into Mexico. There are eight principal gateway cities, including El Paso, across the Rio Grande from Juarez, and Brownsville, across the river from Matamoros.

Four bridges link El Paso to Juarez, Mexico's largest city on the U. S. border. Juarez is an old city, too, with buildings dating back to the 17th century. Shoppers will want to visit the orange-and-blue Juarez Market (*Mercado Juaréz*) and browse. For more information about border crossings and tours, see www.visitelpaso.com.

Across from Texas's southernmost city, Brownsville, is Matamoros, the most historically significant of the Rio Grande border towns. It was the site of the first major battle of the Mexican-American War, and Confederates smuggled contraband cotton across the border there for shipment to European markets. Today its appeal is mostly as a day-trip shopping destination. Like all the Mexican border towns, Matamoros caters to U.S. visitors with gift shops, shopping markets, restaurants, and even festivals. The Expo Fiesta is in June and July, and the Festival Internacional de Otoño is in October. See www.brownsville.org.

It is also possible to get to Mexico by way of Ciudad Acuña from Del Rio (www.drchamber.com), Piedras Negras from Eagle Pass (www.eaglepasstexas.com), Nuevo Laredo from Laredo (www.visitlaredo.com), Reynosa from either Hidalgo or McAllen (www.mcallenchamberusa.com), and Nuevo Progreso from Weslaco (www.weslaco.com).

Borderland:

Cultural distinctions blur and emerge as something unique along the Rio Grande.

Maybe the practice was begun by the likes of Davy Crockett when he came to Texas from Tennessee. Or maybe it was all those Texas cowboys sounding off when they went up the trail to Dodge City. Or maybe it was just the frontier phenomenon of folks being overwhelmed with the bigness of the country and feeling compelled to talk about it.

Early land promoters certainly extolled the virtues of Texas to entice settlers to come, figuring that "braggin' saves advertisin'." At any rate, the habit was established, and Texas residents still have a reputation for bragging about the superiority of all things Texan. The stereotype is one they're even willing to joke about on their own.

There's the story about the old boy who was visiting a friend in New York State. The New Yorker tired of hearing the Texan talk about how much bigger and better everything was back home and drove west toward Buffalo for a view of Niagara Falls.

"There," the New Yorker said, when they reached the falls. "You don't have anything like that down in Texas, do you?" "No, sir," the Texan said, "but we sure have a plumber in Houston who could fix that leak!"

And then there's the one about the Texan whose seatmate on an airline flight was a sweet young thing from Kentucky. She, too, got tired of hearing all the boasting about oil money and Cadillacs and the like and finally said, "Well, you know that we have enough gold in Kentucky at Fort Knox to build a 3-foot-high fence all the way around Texas."

The Texan hardly took a breath before he said, "Well, I tell you what, darlin', y'all go ahead and build it, and, if we like it, we'll buy it!"

Bragging:

Filled with state pride, Texans have earned a reputation for claiming that everything is bigger and better in the Lone Star State.

#1

you know you're in
texas when...
...the Caddy is regarded as art

Stanley Marsh 3 (he thinks the Roman numeral III is pretentious) is an art lover, of sorts. So in 1973 the Texas millionaire commissioned a San Francisco artists' collective called the Ant Farm to create a unique work on his ranch west of Amarillo.

What resulted was the Cadillac Ranch, finished in 1974 and said to represent the "golden age" of American automobiles and the rise and fall of the tailfin. Ten vintage Cadillacs, ranging from a 1949 club coupe to a 1963 sedan, are half buried, grill down, facing west (some claim at the angle of the Great Pyramid of Giza) in a cow pasture.

And Marsh leaves the gate open.

As the Amarillo city limits began encroaching in 1997, the Cadillac Ranch was exhumed from its original location and reburied about 2 miles farther west, but otherwise it remains pretty much the same. Except for the paint jobs. Originally in pastel colors and shiny silver, the cars—most acquired used for an average of $200 apiece—are now covered with spray-painted graffiti.

Over the years, vandals and souvenir hunters have smashed windows and taken chrome, radios, speakers, and doors. The wheels are welded to the axles now to dis-

Cadillac Ranch:

A collection of Cadillacs buried at the same angle as the Great Pyramid surely qualifies as one of the eight wonders of Amarillo.

courage thieves. Marsh is okay with all that, satisfied that the installation is a public sculpture. "We think it looks better every year," he says.

Judge for yourself. The Cadillac Ranch is on old Route 66, south of I–40 between exits 60 and 62.

you know you're in
texas when...
...you're on the king's highway

Driving Highway 21 in Texas is also driving El Camino Real de los Tejas, designated a National Historic Trail in 2004. Most Texans call it the Old San Antonio Road, however, and abbreviate it OSR on road signs, just so you know.

The whole of El Camino Real, generally translated from the Spanish as "the King's Highway," runs about 700 miles from the interior of Mexico to western Louisiana. It has existed for more than 300 years. The currently designated trail extends across a 550-mile-long corridor from the Rio Grande near Eagle Pass and Laredo to Natchitoches, Louisiana, and passes through some of the most spectacular scenery in Texas.

Driving west to east you'll see Spanish missions in San Antonio; beautiful rivers in New Braunfels, San Marcos, and Bastrop; pine forests out of Crockett; Caddo Indian mounds in Alto; and a dozen or more historic small towns such as Nacogdoches and San Augustine.

You'll be following the footsteps of Spanish missionaries, Mexican and Texan armies, early settlers, and individuals such as Kit Carson, Davy Crockett, Jim Bowie, Sam Houston, and Santa Anna, to name a few.

The earliest segments of El Camino Real, originally more a network of trails than a road, were probably links between Indian

El Camino Real:

The oldest road in Texas is a trail through state history.

settlements. During Spanish colonial times it was a major artery for travel and a lifeline for the missions. Spanish ranchers drove cattle along the route, and Moses Austin and his son Stephen brought early settlers into Texas by way of the historic road.

In 1915 the Texas legislature, supported by the Daughters of the American Revolution and other patriotic organizations, appropriated $5,000 to fund a survey that would mark some kind of "official" route.

A surveyor named V. N. Zivley could find little physical evidence of the trail but studied river crossings, topographic features, and old diaries to come up with his best-guess version of the Old San Antonio Road. It was adopted by the Texas legislature as a historic trail in 1929.

you know you're in
texas when...
...some steaks are battered and fried

Most Texans would no doubt list chicken-fried steak as their number one down-home comfort food.

There is no chicken in chicken-fried steak, you understand, and not even a very prime cut of beef. The usual recipe calls for round steak, run through a tenderizer at the meat market or pounded into tender submission with a meat mallet at home. The secret is in the method of cooking.

Like real southern-fried chicken, the steak is dipped in a milk and egg mixture, dredged with seasoned flour, and fried in about a half inch of cooking oil in a cast-iron skillet. Beware of any restaurant that submerges a prebattered, fresh-from-the-freezer cube steak in a deep fryer. That is not the real thing.

Almost as important as the steak is the accompanying cream gravy. Made with the pan drippings, flour, milk or cream, and seasonings, the gravy should be stirred until it is fairly thick, preferably with a wooden spoon, in that same cast-iron skillet. You may want to order it on the side.

Mashed potatoes with a few lumps to prove they're not the instant kind are standard as a side, being good repositories for some of the gravy. And a couple of pieces of thick Texas toast are perfect for sopping up if you're intent on cleaning your plate.

Additional sides may include green beans or black-eyed peas and a salad, but these are considered incidental.

Some folks who seem to be in the know say that you should order chicken-fried steak only from places that have at least four or five pickups parked outside. That may be a good rule to follow.

Otherwise, if you trust *Texas Monthly* magazine's ratings, try the fare at Tony's Southern Comfort in Austin, the Mecca in Dallas, the Barbecue Inn (which offers brown as well as cream gravy) in Houston, or Richard's Chicken in Lubbock for starters.

Chicken-Fried Steak:

This mainstay comfort food in Texas is generally served with cream gravy and mashed potatoes.

Cans of store-bought chili are often labeled chili con carne, as if the spicy stew is all about the hot peppers (chiles) and meat is just an afterthought. That's pretty much the case, at least in Texas. Real Texas chili, according to the purists, has no beans, first of all, and the most important ingredient *is* the peppers—fresh, dried, diced, or powdered.

Trying to trace the history of chili making is like trying to pick out the best recipe: a hopeless quest. Although clearly influenced by Spanish and Mexican cuisine, chili is not an import from Mexico. Texans claim it as their own concoction.

Whether chili as we know it is a product of the Texas trail drives or the invention of the Texas prison system or of the "chili queens" who sold it from carts on Military Plaza in San Antonio doesn't really seem to matter. As long as it's still available in the chili parlors that began to spring up by the Depression years, Texans are happy. The chili was cheap and the crackers were free back then, so it was a very popular dish. It still is.

But enough history. Let's talk about the here and now and where of chili-making competitions. There are chili cook-offs all over the state, but one decides the "world championship." The Terlingua International Chili Championship is held each year on the first Saturday in November in south Texas. Thousands of hungry chili lovers show up to swell the population of the tiny, remote ghost town just northwest of Texas's famed Big Bend National Park.

There are actually two cook-offs at this event. One is sponsored by the Chili Appreciation Society International (www.chili.org/terlingua.html). The other claims to be the Original Terlingua International Frank X. Tolbert–Wick Fowler Memorial Championship Chili Cook-off (www.abowlofred.com). Try saying that with a mouthful of the official state food of Texas!

Chili:

Its recipes are so hotly contested that there are cook-offs all over the state.

you know you're in
texas when...
...some kitchens are built on wheels

It's no wonder Texans take to tailgating—that is, gathering to eat around the back end of a vehicle—with such enthusiasm. There's a pioneering precedent for it: the chuck wagon.

The chuck wagon was invented in 1866 by Texas rancher Charles Goodnight to keep his cowboys fed as they moved cattle up the trail to markets in New Mexico and Colorado. The wagon would move ahead of the herd so the cook could set up camp and have a hot meal ready by the time the trail hands arrived with the cattle.

Goodnight's prototype was built on an Army surplus Studebaker wagon custom fitted with a sloping chuck box on the back. Inside were shelves and drawers to store what the cook would need in the way of dried beans and peas, flour and cornmeal, and so forth to complement the beef and bison that were the mainstays on his menu. The hinged lid of the front of the box folded down to make a worktable.

That same basic design is still in use today by camp cooks, who more often set up on recreational trail rides and outdoor festivals of one kind or another than on cattle drives. The cooking utensil of choice is still the cast-iron Dutch oven, a large, deep pot with a fitted lid. Its slightly recessed center holds live coals so that biscuits, and even the occasional fruit cobbler, can be baked with heat from above and below.

Chuck Wagon:

Invented by Texas rancher Charles Goodnight after the Civil War, this rolling kitchen kept the cowboys fed on long cattle drives.

Folks still gather around the cook fire (no eating off Cookie's table) to swap yarns and sing songs and visit about the day's events while they eat. Sometimes they get to sample the fare in chuck-wagon cook-offs like the one held in conjunction with the National Cowboy Symposium & Celebration in Lubbock each September (www.cowboy.org).

To get a good look at a typical Goodnight-design chuck wagon, visit the Panhandle–Plains Historical Museum in Canyon (www.panhandleplains.org).

Six months after the launch of *Sputnik* and in the midst of the cold war, a tall, lean, lanky 23-year-old Texan showed up in Moscow in 1958 to play the piano. And he played it very well. So well, in fact, that the audience gave him an eight-minute standing ovation and the Soviet judges agreed that he'd won the First International Tchaikovsky Piano Competition.

First, though, they had to ask Premier Nikita Khrushchev for permission to give the first prize to an American since the event was planned to demonstrate the cultural superiority of the Soviets. To his credit, Khrushchev asked the right question: "Is he the best?" "Yes," the judges said. "Then give him the prize!" And so they did.

Van Cliburn came back to the United States to be honored with a ticker-tape parade in New York City and to grace the cover of *Time* magazine as "The Texan Who Conquered Russia." His subsequent recording of Tchaikovsky's Piano Concerto No. 1 became the first classical album to sell a million copies; eventually it went triple platinum.

Born in Louisiana, Cliburn moved with his parents to Kilgore, Texas, when he was six. He had been studying piano with his mother since he was three. (Her teacher had been a student of Franz Liszt.) By the time he was 12, Cliburn had won a state-wide competition and debuted with the Houston Symphony Orchestra. At 17 he entered the Juilliard School, and at 20 he made his Carnegie Hall debut in New York.

But it was his triumph in Moscow that made him, as he said, not just a success but a sensation. He went on to have a busy performing and recording schedule through the 1970s.

In 1962 he became the artistic adviser for the Van Cliburn International Piano Competition, held every four years in Fort Worth. Its prestige now rivals that of the Tchaikovsky Competition.

Cliburn, Van:

Winner of the First International Tchaikovsky Piano Competition in Moscow in 1958, this Texan went on to establish his own piano contest.

Texans are fairly quick to declare an official state version of almost anything.

Since 1989 Texas has had an official state air force, albeit a commemorative one. But the story about it begins much earlier. It was 1951 when Lloyd Nolen, a former World War II Army Air Corps flight instructor, and four of his friends pooled their money to buy a P-51 Mustang. They formed what they first called the Confederate Air Force, a decidedly unofficial group. The CAF kept acquiring vintage airplanes and restoring them. By 1961 there were nine.

In the fall of that same year, the group took on official status as a Texas nonprofit organization with a mission: to restore and preserve World War II–era combat aircraft. Added to the fleet were medium and heavy bombers such as the B-29, B-25, B-17, and B-24.

Today there are more than 140 airplanes in what is known as the Ghost Squadron. CAF moved its headquarters from the Rio Grande Valley to Midland in 1991 and changed its name in 2001. It's now the more politically correct Commemorative Air Force.

The American Airpower Heritage Museum (www.airpowermuseum.org) at the 75-acre CAF headquarters complex in Midland dis-

Commemorative Air Force:

Five veteran pilots started this group, which has amassed one of the most impressive collections of flyable World War II combat aircraft in the country.

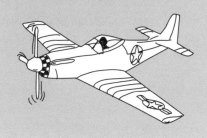

plays World War II artifacts and memorabilia. Visitors can also see anywhere from 14 to 20 aircraft on display at any given time in the CAF hangar. The newest gallery houses the world's largest collection of aviation nose art.

The CAF also brings airplanes to the people in air shows around the country.

Back in 1958, Jack Kilby was a new hire at Texas Instruments in Dallas. He had no vacation time built up, so he was holding down the fort, more or less, at a relatively deserted semiconductor laboratory in July while most other TI employees were on holiday. Kilby no doubt had some time on his hands, and he was working on an idea.

He was trying to figure out how to solve a problem engineers and inventors were calling the "tyranny of numbers"—how to make more of less. Since transistors had replaced the old vacuum tubes in the electronics industry, the challenge was how to get all the various components—sometimes hundreds or thousands of them—wired and connected in a cost-effective way.

Kilby began to sketch out his idea for a working integrated circuit built on a piece of semiconductor material. He had a crude prototype of his chip ready to demonstrate by September. It worked, but the industry was skeptical about its commercial value. Kilby later said that it "provided much of the entertainment at major technical meetings over the next few years."

Even after the military began using the integrated circuit in early computers with the silicon chip in 1961 and in the Minuteman Missile in 1962, there was still no commercial interest. To grab some atten-

tion, Texas Instruments challenged Kilby to use his invention in a handheld calculator that would be as powerful as desktop models. He did, and the success of the integrated circuit was assured.

The most lasting and dramatic impact, however, was in the computer industry. The chip transformed the computer from a bulky, room-size behemoth to the streamlined mainframes, minicomputers, and personal computers we know today.

In 2000 Kilby was awarded the Nobel Prize in Physics, and Texas Instruments has honored him by naming its research and development center in Dallas the Kilby Center. It is said to be the world's most advanced research center for silicon manufacturing.

Computer Chip:

It was the chip that Jack built—Nobel Prize laureate Jack Kilby, that is—that changed the world of computers.

you know you're in
texas when...
...you're eating lunch on a stick

Texans hang on to their traditions, and one they continue to cling to, even in these cholesterol-conscious days, is the corny dog at the state fair. You've just got to have one dunked in mustard and eaten off a stick.

Two brothers, Neil and Carl Fletcher, introduced the deep-fried delight at the 1942 fair. The Fletchers didn't invent the hot dogs coated in cornmeal batter; they got the idea from a street vendor in Dallas back in the 1930s. But they did come up with the idea of putting the hot dogs on a stick and thereby created the ultimate fair food.

The next generation of the family continues to serve Fletcher's Original Corny Dogs at six locations on the fairgrounds each fall, selling more than a half million over the three-plus weeks of the annual event.

Neil's sons, Skip and Bill, run the show now and have made only one significant change over the years: adding a jalapeño cheese corny dog to the menu. They're not interested in expanding the business beyond the run of the fair.

Skip's wife and daughter-in-law, however, have put the Fletcher name on the fast track. They have been peddling the family corny dogs to racing fans at the Texas Motor Speedway north of Fort Worth since

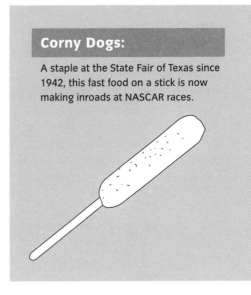

Corny Dogs:

A staple at the State Fair of Texas since 1942, this fast food on a stick is now making inroads at NASCAR races.

the NASCAR track opened in 1999. They've also tried vending at the Dallas Zoo, the Denton Arts & Jazz Festival, and other events around the Dallas and Fort Worth areas.

For tradition's sake, it's still mandatory to eat your corny dog at Fair Park on the midway in the fall.

Find the courthouse squares, and you'll find some of the best examples of architecture the state of Texas has to offer.

Texas has more historic county courthouses than any other state. That could be because Texas has more counties than any other state—254, to be exact. And today more than 225 Texas courthouses that are at least 50 years old still stand. About 80 were built before the turn of the 20th century.

The veteran is "Old Cora," on display in Comanche. This simple split-log, one-room courthouse, built in 1856, takes its name from the town that was the original county seat. When the seat moved to Comanche, the Cora courthouse became a private residence; later it was bought and moved to its current location.

The Clay County Courthouse in Henrietta was built in 1884 and is one of 21 originals still operating in the state. Another of the same vintage is the Parker County Courthouse in Weatherford, certainly much fancier and grander than "Old Cora." The Parker County building even has four clocks on its tower.

One San Antonio architect stayed particularly busy designing courthouses in the late 19th and early 20th centuries. J. Riely Gordon created plans for courthouses in San Antonio, Waxahachie, Sulphur Springs, Marshall, Decatur, and Waco, among other

County Courthouses:

Most of these Texas treasures were built in the late 1800s or early 1900s.

towns, during what might be called the courthouse boom in Texas.

In recent years county residents have rallied to save some of these relics from the past, most notably in Hillsboro. The three-story courthouse there was built in 1890. After a fire gutted it in 1993, all that remained were its limestone walls and iron staircases.

Determined to preserve and restore, Hill County residents and elected officials saw to it that the courthouse was rebuilt by the end of the 1990s. Its clock tower is 70 feet tall and covered with ornate tinwork.

Now the state has a Courthouse Preservation Initiative, which allocates government funds to help rebuild and protect these architectural and historical treasures.

you know you're in
texas when...
...you hit the trail

To tell the truth, the closest some Texans get to a cow is when they pass a milk truck on the freeway. They're likely to define *roundup* as a brand name for a weed killer. But the cowboy mystique lives on in Texas, where trail driving has a legitimate and colorful history.

Although cattle raising and cattle trailing had been around since Spanish colonial times, it was right after the Civil War that enterprising Texans joined in "making the gather." They began rounding up the unbranded maverick cattle that had roamed free while men were fighting away from home during the war years.

Then they had to get the cattle to market. The heyday of trail drives began in 1866 and continued until about 1890. Mounted riders came to be called cowboys. Many of them were boys no more than 18 or 20. Roughly one in three were Mexican or African American; some were actually cowgirls disguising themselves as boys.

They tended mostly longhorns, which were mostly wild, and they spent about six weeks on one of several trails: the Shawnee, the Western, the Goodnight-Loving, or, probably the most famous of all, the Chisholm.

The old trails are crisscrossed now with roads and cities; thus it's hard to imagine six million Texas longhorns herded by hundreds of trail bosses and cowhands following chuck wagons and remudas through lush, green grass. But the state of Texas is making it a little easier for you to recapture the cowboy spirit passed down and preserved in the people and places along at least one trail, the Chisholm.

Starting in Brownsville, you can make your own drive up through Kingsville, Goliad, Victoria, Cuero, Yoakum, San Antonio, and Fort Worth before arriving at Red River Station near Spanish Fort, where Texas cattle crossed the Red River into Oklahoma. That's where Chisholm Trail Memorial Park is.

Before you light out, get the Texas Historical Commission's free Texas Heritage Trails Program brochure and guide. Call (512) 463–6255 or visit www.thc.state.tx.us.

Cowboys and Cattle Trails:

After the Civil War, cowboys herded millions of cattle up major trails from Texas to New Mexico and Kansas.

you know you're in
texas when...
... you know who shot J. R.

Who shot J. R.? The sister-in-law did it in one of the most watched television episodes of one of the longest-running prime-time soap operas of all time.

Originally broadcast in the United States from 1978 to 1991, the hit CBS series *Dallas* counted millions of viewers across the country. It also was one of the first series to be distributed globally, eventually being shown in 95 foreign countries.

In the beginning, however, it had only five episodes. And only after those five garnered impressive ratings did CBS approve 13 more. On the strength of the first full season, the show continued and aired for a total of 356 episodes across 13 seasons. Thus it became the most watched series in the world.

Fort Worth–born Larry Hagman played J. R. Ewing, the villainous oil man, throughout the series. (Hagman's mother, Mary Martin, was also a native Texan. She became a Broadway musical legend in shows like *South Pacific, Peter Pan,* and *The Sound of Music*.)

The majority of the dramatic action was filmed in California studios. But exterior locations were filmed at Southfork Ranch in Plano, a suburb north of Dallas, and made the ranch a tourist mecca. The original owners of the ranch, still in residence when the show began, finally gave up and moved out as more and more *Dallas* fans came to see the place and made requests to have parties and other events there.

Southfork (www.southfork.com) is now a conference and event center, and it still claims to be "America's most famous ranch." It continues to draw tourists nostalgic for the weekly adventures of the oil-rich Ewings, welcoming several hundred thousand visitors each year.

Dallas:

This long-running prime-time soap opera was originally scripted as only a five-part drama.

you know you're in
texas when...
...you're getting a Dell, dude

In the early 2000s a cocky young fellow named Steven (played by actor Ben Curtis) appeared in a series of television and print ads and announced, "Dude, you're gettin' a Dell!" He was referring to Dell computers, of course, products of Dell, Inc., headquartered in Round Rock, near Austin.

The Dell success story centers on the founder and chairman of the company, Michael Dell, a college dropout. Oh, he did get his start in college, sort of. While he was a student at the University of Texas at Austin in 1984, Dell started selling IBM-compatible computers built from stock components. He operated his business out of his dorm room under the name PC's Limited. Business was good.

Nevertheless, his parents urged him to concentrate on his studies. Instead, Dell chose to quit school and focus on his growing business full-time. At the end of its first full year of operation, the company's sales hit $6 million.

By the second year (1985), the company was producing a computer of its own design, the "Turbo PC," and advertising in national computer magazines. Dell's whole idea was to bypass the middleman and sell custom-built personal computers directly to consumers. That turned out to be a breakthrough business model, and now

Dell, Michael:

A college dropout, he used $1,000 to start an Austin business that now reports annual revenues in the billions.

the company is one of the top vendors of personal computers worldwide.

In 1992 Dell became the youngest CEO of a company ever to earn a ranking on the Fortune 500 list, and in 2005 his company ranked first among *Fortune* magazine's "Most Admired Companies."

Chances are if you go to a drive-in diner with a bunch of Texans to get a Coke (generally regarded as a generic term in Texas), someone in the crowd is sure to order a Dr Pepper.

It's more than a matter of taste. It's a matter of state pride, for in the soft drink world, Dr Pepper is a Texas original. Created by a pharmacist in Waco back in 1885, its popularity has grown to the point that it is now one of the top three soft drinks in the United States and the number one noncola.

Once rumored to be made from prune juice (no one is divulging the real formula), Dr Pepper was first advertised as a pick-me-up drink that provided a boost at low-energy times of the day: 10:00 A.M., 2:00 P.M., and 4:00 P.M. Later it was described as "the friendly Pepper upper," and finally the consumer was urged to "be a Pepper."

When pharmacist Charles Alderton first developed his drink, it had no name. Customers would simply call out, "Shoot me a Waco!" Alderton's boss, Wade Morrison, is the one credited with naming the drink after a friend of his, Dr. Charles Pepper. For some reason the period after *Dr* was removed in the 1950s.

In time demand outgrew supply, and Morrison partnered up with the owner of a ginger ale company in Waco to form a Dr

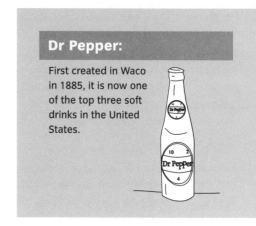

Dr Pepper:

First created in Waco in 1885, it is now one of the top three soft drinks in the United States.

Pepper bottling company in 1891. That company is now the oldest major manufacturer of soft drink concentrates and syrups in the United States.

Already a hit in Texas, Dr Pepper got a big marketing boost when it was introduced—along with hamburger and hot dog buns and ice cream cones—to 20 million people attending the 1904 World's Fair and Exposition in St. Louis.

Nowadays Dr Pepper has its own museum in Waco (www.drpeppermuseum.com), but real connoisseurs may want to drive to Dublin, as the tiny bottling plant there (www.dublindrpepper.com) is the only one that still uses Imperial Pure Cane Sugar in its recipe instead of less expensive corn sweeteners.

You want to see a really big rock? Texas has one. Geologically speaking, it's a batholith: an underground rock formation uncovered by erosion. You can also refer to this exposed pink granite as an exfoliation dome—the second largest one in the United States, in fact. But the locals just call it Enchanted Rock.

Enchanted Rock is not on the road to anywhere, so you have to go looking for it. Take Ranch Road 965 north out of Fredericksburg about 18 miles. You can't miss it. Rising 425 feet above ground, Enchanted Rock is a commanding landmark.

The enchanted part comes from legends created by early Native American inhabitants. The Tonkawas believed that ghost fires flickered at the top of the dome, and they heard weird creaking and groaning there. Geologists have since explained that the noises result from the rock's heating by day and contracting in the cool night.

Part of the 1,643-acre Enchanted Rock State Natural Area, the dome is accessible by two main trails. The shortest and quickest way to the top is by the popular Summit Trail. It's only 0.6 mile long but does call for a fairly steady 425-foot climb. The Loop Trail is a circular 4-mile path that passes around most of the granite peaks.

For experienced rock climbers, there is the sheer Enchanted Rock Fissure.

Impressive as it is, Enchanted Rock is but the tip of the batholith. The underground mass covers 90 square miles.

It's a good idea to call ahead (915–247–3903), as the park closes when it reaches capacity (in terms of parking). That is one way the Texas Parks and Wildlife Department protects the area from overuse.

Enchanted Rock:

This massive pink granite dome may or may not be inhabited by spirits.

Since she was from Texas, a movie studio executive figured Dale Evans could surely rope and ride. So he cast her in a Hollywood western opposite Roy Rogers, the King of the Cowboys. She would go on to become the Queen of the West.

Born in Uvalde in south Texas in 1912, Evans grew up as Frances Octavia Smith, taking her stage name in the 1930s. She set out to become a singer and had some success on the radio and with big bands.

Several moves and three failed marriages after she left Texas, Evans wound up in California under contract with first one movie studio and then another. She finally landed at Republic Studios, where Rogers was already a big star.

Even though she wasn't particularly keen on westerns in the beginning, Evans managed to rope and ride well enough, apparently. She and Rogers made 28 films together, and their on-screen romance became a real-life one. They married on New Year's Eve in 1947.

In 1950 Evans wrote one of the best-known and best-loved cowboy songs of all time, "Happy Trails to You." The story is that she scribbled the lyrics on the back of an envelope and taught the melody to the Sons of the Pioneers 40 minutes before showtime of *The Roy Rogers Show,* a television series that ran until 1957.

A prolific author and songwriter, she wrote several books and wrote or cowrote hundreds of songs, including the Sunday school standard "The Bible Tells Me So."

Among her many honors, the ones of which Evans was most proud included her three stars on the Hollywood Walk of Fame—one each for movies, television, and song—and her induction into the Cowgirl Hall of Fame back in her home state.

In fact, visitors to the National Cowgirl Museum and Hall of Fame (www.cowgirl .net) can't miss Evans, as a life-size image of her flanks the dramatic domed foyer (Roy is on the other side) in Fort Worth. As it turns out, this Texas gal could do a whole lot more than rope and ride.

Evans, Dale:

This Texas-born singer/actress was destined to become the Queen of the West.

you know you're in
texas when...
...the governor wears a petticoat

Texas politics have always been interesting, to say the least, but never more so than in the early part of the 20th century. That's when Ma and Pa Ferguson offered "two governors for the price of one." You see, it happened this way.

James Edward Ferguson, often called "Pa" or "Farmer Jim," served as governor of Texas from 1915 to 1917, when he was impeached on charges of misapplication of funds and other improprieties. Unable to get his own name on the ballot for the 1924 election, he managed the campaign to get his wife elected.

Up to that time, Miriam Amanda Wallace Ferguson had focused her attention on her husband and their two daughters. Perhaps it was that fact, and the combination of her first and middle initials, that led her supporters to call her "Ma." She promised that, if elected, she would follow the advice of her husband and that Texas would therefore be getting "two governors for the price of one."

After defeating a Ku Klux Klan–supported prohibitionist candidate in the Democratic primaries, Ma went on to beat her Republican opponent and become the first woman governor of Texas. In fact, she was the first woman in the whole United States to be elected state governor, but the second to be inaugurated (15 days behind Wyoming's Nellie T. Ross).

Ferguson, Miriam "Ma":

She went from being a first lady to being the first woman governor of Texas.

Ma avoided threatened impeachment over claims that she granted too many pardons and paroles (more than 100 per month, on average) and awarded road contracts to personal friends. She was not renominated in 1926 but did return to the governor's office in 1932 for one more term.

Almost 60 years passed before another woman was elected governor of Texas. That was Ann Richards, who served from 1991 to1995, when she was defeated by an up-and-comer named George W. Bush.

you know you're in
texas when...
... Thanksgiving comes early

Read it and weep, Pilgrims. Texas had one first—Thanksgiving, that is.

Folks in El Paso offer documented evidence that Spanish pioneers held the first Thanksgiving on the banks of the Rio Grande in April 1598, a good 23 years before that one at Plymouth Rock. Here's the story.

Juan de Onate, a silver miner and the wealthiest man in Mexico at the time, was the first successful colonizer of the Southwest. In 1598 he led a trek across Mexican deserts and mountains trying to find a shorter, more direct trail to New Mexico. By the time the sizable procession was nearing the Rio Grande, the travelers had exhausted their provisions and were nearly dead from hunger and thirst.

Fortunately for them, they were met by friendly Manso Indians, and these indigenous people guided them the rest of the way across the desert to the river crossing. To celebrate their safe arrival, the Spaniards held a huge feast and Mass, thus marking, west Texans say, the first Thanksgiving in what is now the United States.

And how do we know this? Because Captain Gasper Perez de Villagra was one of the 600 or so people on the expedition, and he wrote a poem (published in 1610) about the journeys and hardships. El Pasoans today celebrate the anniversary of the first Thanksgiving by acting out Villagra's poem.

First Thanksgiving:

Texans say that conquistadors, not Pilgrims, first gave thanks for their own survival in the New World.

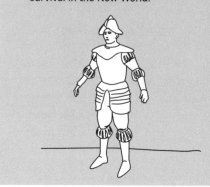

As far as anyone can tell from reading Villagra's account, the 16th-century menu included fish and fowl and cool water from what was then one of the great rivers of North America. Imbibing that last wouldn't be advisable these days.

It is de Onate, by the way, who gets credit for naming El Paso, actually El Paso del Rio del Norte, the Ford of the River of the North.

If you want to join the First Thanksgiving celebration in El Paso, show up at Chamizal National Memorial Park (www.nps.gov/cham) the last Saturday and Sunday in April. But don't drink the water—at least not out of the river.

you know you're in
texas when...
...you celebrate the harvest

Texas is a state that loves its festivals, and it's proud of its produce. So annual harvests are celebrated fruit by fruit and vegetable by vegetable.

The largest agricultural festival in Texas is also one of the oldest. The annual Poteet Strawberry Festival has been going on since 1948. It has more than a dozen areas of continuous family entertainment each April and plenty of opportunities to buy and eat strawberries.

Long recognized as the "Strawberry Capital of Texas," Poteet produces 40 percent of all state strawberries. Festival organizers claim that the annual event draws crowds in excess of 100,000 to the small town located about 30 minutes south of San Antonio.

Two other festivals of note spotlight Texas favorites: pink grapefruit and cantaloupe. The Texas Citrus Fiesta in Mission each January includes lemons and oranges in its lineup, but it is the ruby red grapefruit that is most celebrated. It is, after all, the designated state fruit, and upwards of 10 million 40-pound boxes of Texas reds are exported each year.

Pecos cantaloupes have a similar reputation as being luscious fruits in demand throughout the United States. West Texans say the quality of the melon is derived from a natural combination of alkali soil, western sunlight, and altitude. The Pecos Cantaloupe Festival takes place each August.

Other celebrations of Texas-grown produce include the Rio Grande Valley Onion Festival in Weslaco (April), Texas Blueberry Festival in Nacogdoches (June), Luling Watermelon Thump (June), Texas International Apple Festival in Medina (July), and Black-eyed Pea Jamboree in Athens (October).

At least a couple of fruits get more than one celebration. Peach festivals are held in Weatherford, De Leon, and Teague—all in July. And grape festivals are held in Tow in August and Lodi in September.

Food Festivals:

Texas-grown fruits and vegetables get their own harvest celebrations throughout the state.

texas when...

...couples check the football schedule before they plan the wedding

Rodeo notwithstanding, some Texans recognize only three sports: high school football, college football, and professional football.

Long before the Dallas Cowboys rode into the National Football League in 1960 and became "America's Team," fans were gathering in high school and college stadiums across the state. Even small Texas schools muster six-man and eight-man squads.

Some stadiums have become shrines to the sport and tourist attractions in their own right. The Cotton Bowl, located in Dallas's Fair Park, has been around since 1930. The first Cotton Bowl Classic game pitted Texas Christian University against Marquette University on New Year's Day in 1937. The TCU Horned Frogs won 16 to 6. Until the demise of the Southwest Conference, the annual bowl game matched the winner of that conference with another highly rated team.

More recently, the Cotton Bowl usually gets the number two finisher in the Big 12 Conference and a team from the Southeast Conference. The game is still played on or near January 1.

The University of Texas–University of Oklahoma game, called the Red River Shootout, has an even longer history at the Cotton Bowl. The Longhorns and the Sooners have been playing each other since 1900, consistently in Dallas since 1929 and in the Cotton Bowl since it opened. As of 2006, Texas still led the series.

Both the Dallas Texans (now the Kansas City Chiefs) and the Cowboys played in the Cotton Bowl before Texas Stadium was built in 1971. Daytime guided tours of the newer facility in Irving are available during the season (972–785–4787).

Houston's first professional team, the Oilers (now the Tennessee Titans), played in the Astrodome, completed in 1965. The world's first domed stadium, this "eighth wonder of the world" set a futuristic standard for stadium construction.

Houston's newer NFL team, the Texans, plays in the nearby retractable-roofed Reliant Stadium, built in 2002.

Football:

It's not just the lure of Friday night lights in Texas; football frenzy can last all week.

It's no wonder Fort Worth is still called Cowtown. Having earned that nickname during the height of the cattle drive days after the Civil War, it now celebrates its western heritage at one place in particular: the Stockyards National Historic District.

Already a frequent stop for cattlemen moving herds through the area, Fort Worth earned status as a major cattle-shipping point with the arrival of the Texas and Pacific Railroad in 1876. The opening of various meatpacking companies led to Fort Worth's becoming one of the major beef suppliers in the country.

That lasted until the 1960s, when the Swift and Armour companies closed their doors. By 1976 the Stockyards area was a candidate for renovation; it emerged as one of the most famous and entertaining historic sites in Texas.

These days, tourists stroll the redbrick streets lined with century-old storefronts now housing western wear stores, saloons, eateries, and a hotel. More places to shop and eat are in Stockyards Station, where once there were livestock pens.

The Mission Revival–style Livestock Exchange Building is in the heart of the Stockyards district. It was completed in 1903 and is now home to the North Fort Worth Historical Society's museum. The

Fort Worth Stockyards:

Once the biggest livestock market south of Kansas City, this renovated historic site now draws herds of human visitors.

Stockyards held its last cattle auction in 1992.

Nearby is Cowtown Coliseum, constructed in 1908 to provide a permanent home for the Fort Worth Fat Stock Show. It was the site of the world's first indoor rodeo; later it became a venue for performances by superstars such as Elvis Presley.

And yes, there are still cows in Cowtown. Twice daily, cowboys drive a small herd of 10 to 15 longhorns through the district down Exchange Avenue for no purpose other than to amuse the tourists. The cattle have made the trip so often you figure they could do it on their own, but that just wouldn't be the same.

If presentation is everything, then Frito pie would surely win in the category of unique serving ideas. Here's the recipe: Slit open the side of a bag of Frito corn chips—the individual-size bag—and dump in a ladleful or two of chili on top of the chips. Add grated cheese and chopped onion, and you're done. Unless you want jalapeño peppers.

Eat the whole artery-clogging concoction right out of the sack. But be fairly speedy about it, or the chips will get soggy. It's important to use real Fritos because they stay firmer longer than any corn chip substitutes.

Although some folks in New Mexico claim that a woman working at a Woolworth's in Santa Fe came up with the idea for Frito pie, all Texans and most food historians give credit to Elmer Doolin's mother.

The story is that Doolin, a San Antonio ice cream maker, ate a nickel bag of corn chips one day in 1932 in a local cafe and liked them so well that he paid $100 for the recipe, the converted potato ricer used to make them, and the 19 retail accounts for the product.

He named the chips Fritos and moved his operation to Dallas. It was there that his mother, Daisy, came up with the idea for Frito pie. Its popularity peaked in the

Frito Pie:

Arguments from New Mexico notwithstanding, Texans claim that their corn chip, chili, onion, and cheese conglomeration was the first.

1960s, when it was a staple item in almost every high school football and basketball game concession stand in the state. It's still a great favorite at sports events, at burger stands and diners, and even at some restaurants, although it's generally served in bowls there.

According to a 2006 AAA *Texas Journey* magazine article, the basic version is still available at places like Amarillo's Golden-Light Cafe (806–374–0097) and Austin's Texas Chili Parlor (512–472–2828).

There are remnants of at least 15 frontier forts in Texas, but 8 of them—featured on the Texas Forts Trail (www.texasfortstrail .com) in the west-central part of the state—get the most attention. Of those 8, Fort Concho is the best preserved. As a matter of fact, it's the best preserved western fort in the United States.

Located along the banks of the Concho River in San Angelo, Fort Concho was established in 1867. Many historians consider it one of the best examples of post–Civil War frontier military architecture west of the Mississippi. Credit the skill of German craftsmen from Fredericksburg who built most of the stone structures with pecan-wood beams and rafters.

Among the many regiments it housed was the famed 10th Cavalry unit of African-American soldiers, better known as the Buffalo Soldiers.

The fort was abandoned as a military post in 1889; the buildings were then occupied as family residences or by commercial enterprises, so they didn't fall into disrepair. In 1929 restoration of the post began, the preservation efforts spearheaded by the citizens of San Angelo.

Now a National Historic Landmark, Fort Concho boasts 23 original and restored structures and 4 living-history units. Several special events take place during the year, climaxing with Christmas at Fort Concho in December. For more information, call (325) 481–2646 or visit www.fort concho.com.

If you want to see the other seven sites on the Texas Forts Trail, allow several days and figure on more than one tank of gas. You'll be driving about 450 miles, looking for the towns of Jacksboro (Fort Richardson), Graham (Fort Belknap), Throckmorton (Fort Griffin), Abilene (Fort Phantom Hill), Albany (Fort Chadbourne), Menard (Fort McKavett), and Mason (Fort Mason).

Frontier Forts:

Established as outposts to protect American settlers moving west, these relics are now reminders of a colorful period in Texas history.

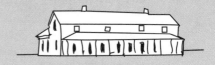

When Texans see the light, it's sometimes a ghost light, or so folks say.

Lights appear in Anson near the cemetery, reportedly caused by the specter of a woman looking for her lost son. The Saratoga lights, rumored to be the spirit remains of a decapitated railroad worker, show up among the pine trees in the Big Thicket. Probably the best-known ghost-light legend is Brit Bailey's down in Brazoria County. His light still roams Bailey's Prairie looking for a jug of whiskey.

But the Marfa lights have them all beat as a Texas tourist attraction. It could be Marfa's marketing or simply the reliability of the lights there. They show up fairly predictably just after sundown on Mitchell Flat, about 9 miles east of Marfa.

Storytellers offer more than one legend to explain the Marfa lights. The most prevalent suggest the presence of the ghost of an Apache chief named Alsaste. One story says he raided into Mexico once too often and was executed. Another says Alsaste got separated from his people and roams the hills lighting fires. Yet another leaves him guarding gold in a cave.

The locals agree that these theories make about as much sense as ones put forward by scientists investigating the phenomenon. The sightings began in the 1800s, so it's unlikely that automobile headlights or house lights are the cause. Swamp gas, ball lightning, and phosphorescent jackrabbits don't really offer satisfactory answers either. The Marfa lights can't really be explained. They are simply there.

And aren't the enterprising folks in Marfa glad? Tourism now vies with ranching as an income source in the area. The Texas Highway Department provides a public viewing site, and there's a Marfa Lights Festival every September.

The viewing area is on Highway 90 about halfway between Marfa and Alpine. Visitors look east of the Chianti Mountains to see different colored lights rise, fall, dip, and dance in the dark of night. For more information, contact the Marfa Chamber of Commerce at (915) 729–4942.

Ghost Lights:

Those at Marfa get the most attention, but there are eerie illuminations all over Texas.

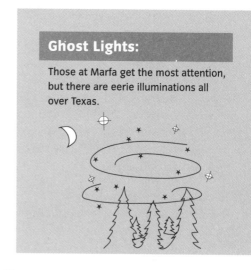

In 1955 Marfa was a ranching town of maybe 3,600 people. That summer an army of technicians, cameramen, and various other kinds of workers descended on it. They built a huge mansion out on the plains—a house with no rooms, just a facade. They set up miniature oil derricks all over the prairie and took every available room in the Hotel Paisano downtown.

The actors came later to stay in rented houses. Rock Hudson and Elizabeth Taylor were already very well known, but James Dean was starring in only his third movie. They were in Texas to film *Giant,* an epic story about Texas adapted from Edna Ferber's best-selling novel.

Some Texans resented Ferber's portrayal of what they believed were too many negatives about the state, but most have come, over the years, to embrace what has been called "the archetypal Texas movie." The rest of the world got a glimpse of cattle barons and oil-rich landowners dealing with social and economic change and thought that's who Texans were or should be.

At a time when most movies were filmed almost entirely in California, most of the exterior shots for *Giant*—particularly the ones in front of the Reata ranch house—were filmed on location on a real ranch near Marfa. The interior scenes, however, were shot on the Warner Bros. lot in Burbank.

Giant:

Edna Ferber's best-selling novel was the source for George Stevens' epic movie.

For years the remains of the Reata stood on the Texas ranch land as reminders of the summer "when stars fell on Marfa." Not much is left now except autographed pictures in the Hotel Paisano, where a 50th-anniversary showing of the movie took place in the summer of 2005.

Giant won the Academy Award for director George Stevens; Hudson and Dean were nominated as best actor and Mercedes McCambridge as best supporting actress. It turned out to be Dean's last movie—he was killed in a car accident before *Giant* was released.

You don't order shrimp in Texas. You order Gulf shrimp, preferably in one of the coastal communities stretching along the Gulf of Mexico from Port Arthur to Port Isabel. Of course, there are bay shrimp, too, if you want to get technical, but they account for only about 18 percent of the total annual catch, and you probably couldn't tell the difference.

Shrimping is the most important commercial fishing industry in Texas, and since the 1950s, Texas has been one of the big three producers of shrimp, along with Alaska and Louisiana. Truth be told, it was some of those neighboring Louisiana shrimpers who really got the Texas Gulf industry going right after World War II, when they moved their base of operations to the west.

Before that, most shrimping had been carried out in the Texas coastal bays, where commercial netting dates back to the mid-19th century or before. Maybe that's because bay shrimpers, who have smaller boats that typically can be manned by two men (sometimes only one), have less overhead. And they can be home by dark.

Gulf shrimpers, on the other hand, must have bigger trawlers and larger crews, and they may fish for up to three weeks before returning to port. Sometimes they must fish at night if they are going after the noc-

Gulf Shrimp:

Fresh off the boat and cooked to order, these tasty crustaceans are menu specials along the Texas Gulf coast.

turnal brown or Brazilian shrimp. The work is hard and sometimes dangerous, and the industry has had its economic problems, especially since 1979: prohibition of fishing in Mexican waters, rising fuel costs, increasing competition, and regulations to prevent the killing of sea turtles.

Still, consumer demand and the availability of shrimp in the Gulf of Mexico and in Texas bays keep shrimping viable as an industry. And that's good, because there's nothing better than an order of boiled Gulf shrimp with red sauce. Unless it's grilled Gulf shrimp on a skewer or fried Gulf shrimp with a side of cole slaw and some hush puppies.

you know you're in
texas when...
...rock stars wear glasses

No city is prouder of one of its own than Lubbock is of singer/songwriter Buddy Holly. There's a larger-than-life-size statue downtown of the bespectacled musician playing his Fender Stratocaster guitar. There are also a park bearing his name, a Buddy Holly Walk of Fame, and the Buddy Holly Center, located in the historic Fort Worth and Denver Railroad Depot.

Holly was born in Lubbock on September 7, 1936. He was named Charles Hardin, but his mother said that seemed like too much name for such a little baby. So she started calling him Buddy. And Buddy he stayed.

He recorded more than 100 songs during his short career, including hits like "Peggy Sue" and "That'll Be the Day." He and his band, the Crickets, influenced many young rock-and-rollers, including two lads from Liverpool, England—John Lennon and Paul McCartney—who decided to call their group the Beatles.

When Holly and the Crickets toured England in 1958, McCartney watched them perform on the *Sunday Night at the Paladium* television program. He said he was watching to see which chords Holly played and where he placed his guitar capo.

Guitar licks and song lyrics aside, even Holly's physical appearance set him apart, with his black horn-rimmed glasses and three-button Ivy League jackets. His glasses, his guitar, and other memorabilia are now on display in the Buddy Holly Exhibition in the Buddy Holly Center (www.buddyhollycenter.org).

Holly died in a plane crash in 1959 on his way to Fargo, North Dakota, after finishing a concert in Clear Lake, Iowa, when he was only 22. His memory and his status as a rock-and-roll legend are assured, however, through his music, through movie and musical productions, and certainly through the efforts of his hometown to honor him.

Holly, Buddy:

His short but influential life made him a rock music legend.

At one time it was Gilley's in Pasadena, just southeast of Houston, that was described as "the most Texan of them all, the biggest, brawlingest, loudest, dancingest, craziest joint of its kind ever." So said Bob Claypool in his 1980 book about the honky-tonk made famous in the movie *Urban Cowboy*.

Gilley's burned to the ground in 1990. In 1981 Billy Bob's Texas opened in Fort Worth and now claims to be the world's largest honky-tonk (www.billybobstexas .com). These two are the ones you still hear about most, but they are latecomers.

The history of Texas dance halls goes back to the late 1800s, when German and Czech immigrants built community halls. These structures were for family outings, not just for couples bent on doing some two-stepping or line dancing while a band plays "Cotton-Eyed Joe."

Folks back then were more likely to listen to accordion music than to guitars and fiddles, and they sipped home-brewed beers instead of Lone Star longnecks. And there were no mechanical bulls in the place.

Claiming to be the oldest dance hall in Texas is Gruene Hall (www.gruenehall.com) in the town of Gruene, just outside New Braunfels and not far from San Antonio. Established in 1878, the hall reopened in its second life in 1979 and is more generically country-western than German these days.

Arkey Blue's Silver Dollar Saloon (830–796–8826) didn't come along until the 1930s, but it sits right in the middle of "the cowboy capital of Texas," if you believe Bandera's slogan. From Ernest Tubb to Willie Nelson, Arkey's has played host to some of the country music greats.

Then there's the Broken Spoke (www .brokenspokeaustintx.com). It's been in Austin since 1964 and was built with those old-time dance halls in mind. Starting with his boyhood hero Bob Wills, owner James White has booked most of the big names in country music.

As part of the 25th anniversary of the place, White opened a room filled with photos, hats, and other items related to country music; he calls it the "Tourist Trap Room."

Honky-tonks:

Live country music draws crowds to do some two-stepping or line dancing, or maybe even some waltzing while they're at it.

you know you're in
texas when...
...you see larger-than-life heroes

Sam Houston was tall, judged to be somewhere between 6 feet, 2 inches and 6 feet, 6 inches. But the statue in Huntsville honoring him is way taller than that. Huntsville native David Adickes turned 60,000 pounds of concrete and steel into a 67-foot likeness of Houston you can see from more than 6 miles away. It is the world's largest statue of any American hero.

The fact is, it's hard to go anywhere in Huntsville without being reminded of its famous onetime resident. There's Sam Houston State University, for starters, and nearby is Sam Houston National Forest. Lake Raven uses the name given to Houston by the Cherokees.

All this notoriety in Huntsville may seem strange when you remember that it is the city of Houston that is named for the man. But Huntsville is the city in which he chose to settle down at the end of his political career and the place where he died. He is buried in Oakwood Cemetery there.

There is probably no more colorful or controversial figure in Texas history. Houston got to Texas by way of Virginia and Tennessee, just in time for the revolution. After signing the Texas declaration of independence from Mexico, he became commander in chief of the Texas forces.

He actually retreated from the advance of General Santa Anna's Mexican army but

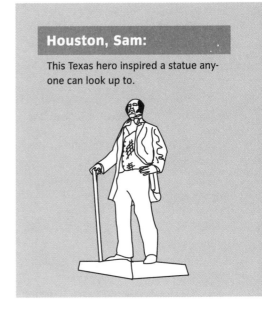

Houston, Sam:

This Texas hero inspired a statue anyone can look up to.

then stood his ground at San Jacinto and won that decisive battle. Twice president of the new Republic of Texas, he was later governor when Texas became a state.

He was removed from the governor's office when Texas seceded from the Union and Houston refused to sign an oath of allegiance to the Confederate States. That's when he went home to Huntsville.

For additional information about him and the area, contact the Huntsville Chamber of Commerce at (800) 289–0389 or visit www.huntsvilletexas.com.

She's been called "the best white blues singer in American musical history" and "the greatest female singer in the history of rock 'n' roll." She did not read music but spent her adolescent years listening to recordings of blues greats like Odetta, Bessie Smith, and Willie Mae Thornton.

Probably no Texan better personified the hard-living, hard-drinking, post-beatnik hippie lifestyle of the 1960s than Janis Joplin, but she had to leave Texas to do it.

Born in the coastal oil-refining town of Port Arthur in 1943, she graduated from high school there and eventually took classes at Lamar State University and at the University of Texas in Austin. During those years she began to rebel against the norms of social acceptance she couldn't quite meet and turned to music as her outlet.

Joplin hitchhiked to California in 1963. There she found success first with a band called Big Brother and the Holding Company, especially when they played the Monterey International Pop Festival in 1967. The raspy, raw intensity of her voice and her flamboyant stage presence got the attention of audience and music critics alike.

Joplin went on to put together two bands of her own and to play at the historic Woodstock Music and Art Fair in 1969. Throughout her career she experimented with drugs and battled an addiction to

Joplin, Janis:

Inducted into the Rock and Roll Hall of Fame in 1995, this Texas-born blues-rock singer lived fast and died young.

alcohol, often appearing on stage with a bottle of Southern Comfort. She died from an accidental overdose of heroin in a Los Angeles hotel room in the fall of 1970. She was only 27.

Her last album, released posthumously in 1971, was her most successful. Titled simply *Pearl* (her nickname), it reached number one on the *Billboard* charts, as did the single "Me and Bobby McGee," written for her by fellow Texan Kris Kristofferson.

In 1979 *The Rose,* a hit film based loosely on her life and starring Bette Midler, premiered in Los Angeles. Joplin also has been the subject of several books and documentaries. In 1988 her hometown folks unveiled a bust of her that now sits in the Port Arthur library.

you know you're in
texas when...
...the most famous Jordan didn't play basketball

Houston-born Barbara Jordan was quick to point out that she began her political career as a "stamper and addresser" of envelopes. And that was true. She was a volunteer in John F. Kennedy's campaign for president in 1960.

But it didn't take long for that magnificent, rich voice of hers to be heard. It happened this way: She went as a volunteer worker to a voter registration rally at a church in Harris County. The speaker for the evening didn't show up, and Jordan offered to speak in her place. Her stamp-licking days were over.

Certainly she was capable of speaking, as she had both the heritage and the training. Her father was a Baptist preacher, her mother a great orator as well. Jordan had a law degree and years of debate experience herself.

In the years that followed, Jordan continued to speak and rack up any number of firsts. But success was not immediate. She ran unsuccessfully twice for the Texas State Senate before finally winning a seat in 1966. That victory made her the first black member of that body since 1883 and the first black woman ever. In 1972 she became the first African-American woman from the South to be elected to the United States Congress.

When Jordan gave the keynote address and nominated Jimmy Carter at the Democratic National Convention in 1976, she became the first African-American keynoter. In 1992 she was again the keynote speaker and nominated Bill Clinton, who awarded her the Presidential Medal of Freedom in 1994.

In the last stage of her career, Jordan was a professor at the Lyndon B. Johnson School of Public Affairs in Austin. She died in 1996.

Jordan, Barbara:

A dynamic orator, she counted several firsts in her political career.

It ain't over 'til it's over. That was certainly true of the Civil War in Texas. In the days before cell phones and CNN, no one got word to soldiers in south Texas that the war had ended. So they kept fighting.

The last land battle of the Civil War was fought at Palmito Ranch near Brownsville on May 13, 1865, and the Confederates won. That was more than a month after Lee surrendered at Appomattox.

Even later came good tidings of freedom to the 250,000 slaves in Texas. It wasn't until June 19, 1865, in Galveston that a Union officer read the general order making their freedom official. So that day—now referred to as "Juneteenth"—became their emancipation day. Anniversary celebrations began in 1866 and have continued off and on ever since.

Early observances in particular had a feel and significance similar to those on the Fourth of July, with lots of public speaking and the reading of the Emancipation Proclamation. At first, Juneteenth was strictly a Texas celebration. Then, as black Texans began to migrate to neighboring states, they took Juneteenth with them, and its impact continued to spread.

Juneteenth festivities initially were relegated to the outskirts of towns, so black groups began to collect funds and pur-

chase land for their celebrations. A common name for these sites was Emancipation Park, and examples still exist in cities like Houston and Austin.

Since 1980 Juneteenth has been a state holiday. That's when the 66th legislature declared June 19 "Emancipation Day in Texas." It continues to get attention outside the state, too.

Juneteenth:

From its Galveston origin in 1865, this celebration of the ending of slavery has spread beyond the state of Texas.

you know you're in
texas when...
...the pickin' and singin' start

What do you do when you run out of room in the auditorium? You move to the ranch. At least that's what the organizers of the Kerrville Folk Festival did, and it's been an outdoor event ever since.

When Rod Kennedy founded the festival back in 1972, it was held in the 1,200-seat Kerrville Municipal Auditorium. More than twice that many music fans showed up to hear 13 performers. The next year 5,600 people jammed the auditorium to hear five concerts over three nights. That's when Kennedy bought the ranch.

Oh, it's not really much of a ranch by Texas standards—only 60 acres—but it has served to corral the crowds in the years since.

Kennedy named his place Quiet Valley Ranch, possibly to keep from scaring the neighbors. But it's doubtful that the valley is all that quiet during what is now the 18-day run of the festival each May. More than 100 musicians perform during a schedule of 11 six-hour concerts, and the crowds keep growing. Many of the 30,000-plus fans these days choose to stay at the campgrounds on the ranch, where impromptu songfests have become a trademark of the festival.

From the beginning, folk music greats like Peter Yarrow (of Peter, Paul, and Mary) and

Kerrville Folk Festival:

The largest festival of its kind in the United States, it celebrates singer/songwriters.

National Fiddling Champion Dick Barrett have come. Other festival performers who have become well known—Willie Nelson, Lyle Lovett, Nanci Griffith, and Lucinda Williams, for example—have brought a Texas country flavor to the music.

The common thread is that they are all songwriters as well as performers. The Kerrville Folk Festival is now America's largest and longest-running celebration of original songwriters, and it draws performers and fans from around the world.

Quiet Valley Ranch is 9 miles south of Kerrville. For more information, call (830) 257–3600 or visit www.kerrville-music.com.

It all started back in 1940, when a Kilgore College dean was looking for a way to attract more female students to the campus. He was also hoping to keep people in their seats during football game halftimes.

So he brought in Gussie Nell Davis. She had already established a high school drum-and-bugle corps called the "Flaming Flashes" in Greenville. The dean gave her free rein, and she gave Kilgore the Rangerettes, the first women's precision drill team in the world.

Davis was a demanding director, calling for perfectly executed routines. Her credo was simple: Rangerettes don't make mistakes. Despite such pressure, female students tried out and trained. They learned choreographed routines, including the group's trademark high kick. The performers became popular locally. Then their fame began to spread.

The Rangerettes traveled to New Orleans to perform at a convention, and they appeared in "bond shows" during World War II. Later came trips to the Sugar Bowl and Macy's Thanksgiving Day Parades. They have appeared at the Cotton Bowl Classic in Dallas each year since 1951.

The Texas State Society for the inauguration celebration of President George W. Bush even invited them to Washington, D.C., twice. They performed at both Texas Black Tie and Boots Balls and were one of the few groups to participate in both inaugural parades.

Davis retired in 1979 and died in 1993, but still the women come. Only 48 members actually perform at one time, although normally 65 students make up the team. They still wear basically the same red, white, and blue costume: blouse, arm gauntlets, belt, short circular skirt, hat, and boots.

In 1979 Kilgore College opened a Rangerette Showcase in its physical education building. It features costumes, props, and other memorabilia. A theater in the building shows films and slide shows of Rangerette performances. For more information, see www.rangerette.com.

Kilgore Rangerettes:

These high-steppers pioneered the field of dancing drill teams.

you know you're in
texas when...
... you're hanging out on Sixth Street

With a Texan's typical lack of humility, Austin claims to be the "Live Music Capital of the World." You can hear a great deal of that music by walking up and down Sixth Street.

Especially on weekends, streams of people course up and down Sixth. The 7-block stretch between Congress Avenue and Interstate 35 attracts university students, yuppies, suburbanites, and out-of-town visitors. You'll also see politicians, the occasional film star, and some pretty interesting local street folk. They come mostly for the eclectic mix of live music pouring out of the bars and clubs that line both sides of the street. Jazz, blues, country, rock, hip-hop—you name it, you'll hear it.

This melting pot of music and humanity really boils during the annual South by Southwest Festival (www.sxsw.com) in March. Since 1987 the music part of the festival (it showcases filmmakers as well) has attracted thousands of musicians and producers to Austin. For music fans there is a nearly 24-hour onslaught of live music showcases, parties, and panels.

Not all the musical acts can fit in the venues on Sixth Street, so nearby streets accommodate the overflow, and some musicians play in Waterloo Park. Pretty much the whole downtown is jumping during the festival run.

Live Music Capital of the World:

That's Austin's slogan, and the city tries to live up to the claim.

Another major festival is the Austin City Limits (www.aclfestival.com), held each September since 2002 in Zilker Park. Named after the popular public television show, this event is a weekend-long celebration of mostly rock and country sounds.

Other somewhat offbeat (pun intended) music festivals are springing up, too: the Heart of Texas Quadruple Bypass Music Festival (www.texasrockfest.com), Austin Marley Festival (www.austinreggaefest .com), and Jerry Garcia Birthday Festival (www.jerrygarciabdayfestival.moonfruit .com), to name a few.

No one is quite sure who designed the lone star flag that first flew over the Republic of Texas and then became the state flag. It's a matter of record, however, that Senator William H. Wharton proposed its adoption for the republic in 1838.

The familiar red, white, and blue design was actually the second official flag of the republic. The first, adopted by the Texas Congress late in 1836, also had a single star, but that star was gold and was centered on "an azure ground." No one is sure who designed it either.

What is certain is that the five-pointed star made prominent in those early flags has become a favorite symbol in Texas. It is part of the state seal and looms large atop the state outline on the 2004 commemorative Texas quarter.

A unique nine-pointed star that nevertheless appears to have only five points when viewed from any angle sits atop the San Jacinto Monument. A 35-foot-tall bronze star is an eye-catcher in front of the Bob Bullock Texas State History Museum in Austin.

The proper finial on poles used to display the state flag, by the way, is either a spearhead or—you guessed it—a star.

And, of course, there's the state nickname, one of the most recognized in the country.

Lone Star:

A recognized symbol since the days when Texas was a republic, it is now part of the state nickname, flag, seal, and lots of other stuff.

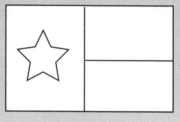

Texas is officially the Lone Star State, although other nicknames have been suggested through the years. Among them are the Beef State, the Banner State, the Blizzard State, the Jumbo State, and the Super-American State. Understandably, none really caught on.

you know you're in
texas when...
...you see the herd a-comin'

Texas is big on declaring official state icons of one kind or another, and it's not surprising that the official state large mammal is the longhorn. Popular as it is now, it was once threatened with extinction.

After railroads and barbed-wire fences pretty well put a stop to the trail drives, the hardy longhorn was phased out. By the 1920s longhorns were being replaced by or cross-bred with cattle that developed faster and were more suited to fenced ranges. But for the efforts of a few men, the longhorn might have been bred out of existence.

In 1927 two U.S. Forest Service rangers took on the task of preserving Texas longhorns by collecting a small herd of breeding stock in south Texas. They moved them to a refuge—not in Texas, but in Oklahoma. Then they established another herd in another refuge, this time in Nebraska.

Eventually, after those out-of-state wildlife refuge herds increased to several hundred, the Forest Service began to sell off surplus animals in annual sales. Cattlemen bought them first as curiosities but soon rediscovered the traits that had made the longhorns so well suited for those long-ago trail drives in the first place: longevity, fertility, resistance to disease, ease of calving, and ability to thrive on marginal pastures.

It helps that today's diet-conscious population is clamoring for lean beef. And at least one burnt-orange longhorn at a time will find steady work as Bevo, the mascot for the University of Texas in Austin.

The official Texas longhorn herd is back home, scattered among a number of state parks. For more information, contact Texas Parks and Wildlife at (800) 792–1112 or visit www.tpwd.state.tx.us/park/.

Longhorns:

Once on the brink of extinction, these Texas icons are back to stay.

If you set out to find Luckenbach, be fore-warned that souvenir hunters keep stealing the road signs. So you're on your own.

The small town, made most famous by a 1977 hit song by Waylon Jennings and Willie Nelson, sits on both sides of Ranch Road 1376. Surrounded by huge live oaks and two creeks, it's a little over 13 miles from Fredericksburg in southeastern Gillespie County.

"Let's go to Luckenbach, Texas, with Waylon and Willie and the boys," the song says. It advocates swapping coat and tie for boots and jeans and getting "back to the basics of love."

There's no doubt that Luckenbach is a back-to-basics kind of place. Established in 1849 as a trading post, the town took its name from an early German settler. By the 1970s, however, it was pretty much a ghost town. That's when Hondo Crouch bought it.

Crouch, a humorist and folklorist and one-time champion swimmer, saw a newspaper ad offering a town for sale, population 3. He and some associates bought the 10-acre community, and Crouch became self-proclaimed mayor and "clown prince."

From the start, his tongue was in his cheek as he made his town a spoofing foil for the Texas White House down the road apiece on the LBJ Ranch. Crouch staged hug-ins, a

Luckenbach Great World's Fair, an annual Mud Daubers' Day, and a Non-Buy Centennial Celebration. "Everybody is somebody in Luckenbach," he used to say.

The town came with several buildings, but two have washed down the creek in recent floods. The original country store is still there, as is the dance hall. That's where some of the biggest names in country music have made concert appearances, Jennings and Nelson included.

Crouch is gone now. He died in 1977 and had his ashes scattered in Luckenbach. A small statue of him sits in front of the country store, and that's where most visitors have their pictures taken. For more information, call (830) 997–3224 or (888) 311–8990 or visit www.luckenbachtexas.com.

Luckenbach:

This tiny town gained fame in 1977 with the release of a hit recording by Waylon Jennings and Willie Nelson.

you know you're in
texas when...
...the sky's the limit

There was a time when the area around Clear Lake, about 30 miles south of Houston, was mostly open prairie, but not anymore. Now it's full of housing developments, apartment complexes, motels, and shopping centers. And NASA.

The National Aeronautics and Space Administration picked the southeast Harris County location out of 20 candidates investigated by a site survey team. Some say it didn't hurt any that native Texan Lyndon B. Johnson was vice president at the time. That was back in 1961.

By 1965 the Manned Space Center was up and running in time to provide mission control for *Gemini 4,* and it has been part of the drama of space flight ever since. Who can forget "Houston, we've had a problem here," uttered when *Apollo 13* survived an explosion in 1970? With help from folks on the ground, the crippled command module made it back to earth with only 15 minutes of power to spare.

In 1973, the year of LBJ's death, the name of the facility was changed to the Lyndon B. Johnson Space Center. It is one of nine NASA field installations and home base for the nation's astronauts.

It's a fun place to visit, too. The Space Center Houston visitor center was designed by Walt Disney Imagineering and opened in

Lyndon B. Johnson Space Center:

Originally known as the Manned Spacecraft Center, this facility is one of nine NASA field installations and home base for the nation's astronauts.

1992. Visitors can tour mission control and astronaut-training facilities, take a look at historic spacecraft and displays, watch an IMAX movie shot in space, and explore a museum of the American space program. For more information, call (281) 244–2100 or visit www.spacecenter.org.

you know you're in
texas when...
...you understand that *Lonesome Dove* is not a bird

Larry McMurtry loves books—and not just the writing of them either. Oh, he's written plenty, more than 30 volumes at last count, but he also collects books. That passion for collecting led him to turn his longtime place of residence, Archer City, into a book town.

A book town is one in which the main business is a bookstore. McMurtry started the first bookstore in Archer City in 1987 and called it The Blue Pig (the only explanation for the name is that his partner liked pigs). When that store outgrew its space, McMurtry moved it and changed the name to Booked Up. It now occupies four buildings downtown and is the biggest business in Archer City. According to the *Texas Travel Guide,* it also contains the largest collection of antiquarian books in the country.

That means McMurtry's own books are not sold there, although there is a display of memorabilia related to his Pulitzer Prize–winning novel *Lonesome Dove.*

One of the most successful authors to come out of Texas in recent years, McMurtry was born in Wichita Falls and grew up on a ranch outside Archer City. Most of his books are set in Texas.

Book lovers and other tourists who come to Archer City are not likely to get McMurtry's autograph, even if he does

McMurtry, Larry:

This award-winning novelist, essayist, screenwriter, and book lover grew up on a ranch outside Archer City.

happen to be in the store, which is located down the street from the courthouse. When he's there he is working, not autographing. "I can't get anything done if I sell my own books or autograph books that people bring in," he says.

Visitors to Booked Up also should not expect precise cataloging stored on a computer. According to the store's Web site (www.bookedupac.com), the books are arranged "Erratically/Impressionistically/Whimsically/Open to Interpretation." It's a place to browse and make discoveries. Just the way McMurtry likes it.

you know you're in
texas when...
...you'll take shade wherever you can find it

Finding shade under a mesquite tree "is like dipping water with a sieve." So said a traveler in Texas way back in the 1840s. That's because the mesquite is one of the last trees to leaf out in the spring. And its leaves are so delicate and feathery that they don't block out much sun anyway.

What the mesquite does do, however, is take more than its fair share of water through its extensive root system. Its taproot can grow as deep as 25 to 65 feet hunting for the water table. Mesquites also have sharp, hard-as-nails thorns—up to 2 inches long—that can injure cattle and horses. Not to mention cowhands.

Texas farmers and ranchers have declared war on what they consider to be a noxious weed. Even so, 76 percent of all the mesquite in the United States grows in Texas.

What's it good for, this hardy plant that can range in size from a squatty, misshapen bush to a 40- to 50-foot-tall tree? Well, it's a legume, a nitrogen-fixing plant that can enrich the soil, for one thing. And its wood is prized by outdoor grill cooks for the flavor it imparts to smoked meats and fish.

Moreover, many artisans and furniture makers choose mesquite wood for its deep colors, rich patina, and interesting irregularities. It's also a hardwood, as hard as hickory and harder than oak and maple.

Seven varieties of mesquite grow in Texas, but the most common is the honey mesquite. It is found in all regions of the state except deep east Texas. There's even a National Champion Honey Mesquite growing on a ranch in Real County in south-central Texas. It measures 172 inches in circumference and is 55 feet tall, according to the Texas Forest Service's Big Tree Registry. Its 89-foot crown spread produces the most shade anybody's going to get from a mesquite.

Mesquite Tree:

Hated by some but loved by others, this ubiquitous plant grows in almost all regions of Texas.

Former Texas governor Bill Clements knew a good author when he read one, and he had read James Michener. Clements decided that Michener was just the man to write a book about Texas, giving it the sweeping breadth and scope of his epic style.

Michener agreed to visit Texas in the early 1980s, but he made it clear that if he decided to write a book about the state, it would be his idea—not a concession to the governor. Furthermore, it would be the complete story of Texas, not some public relations pitch that would necessarily make the state tourism people happy.

Michener decided to write the book. As was his practice, he moved to the location while doing the research. He and his wife, Mari, settled in Austin, and he worked out of an office provided by the University of Texas. By 1985 he had produced his book, simply titled *Texas*. It was a big book— 1,096 pages long—and it became a best seller.

The Micheners became Texans, deciding to stay in Austin. In 1992 James wrote his personal memoirs, *The World Is My Home,* and that was true. In his lifetime he had visited all seven continents and sailed all seven seas, but he chose to make Texas his final residence.

Michener brought more than literary recognition to his adopted state, although the literary legacy lives on through the James A. Michener Center for Writers at the University of Texas. He also left 376 pieces of art to the university; they constitute the Mari and James A. Michener Collection of Twentieth-Century American Art in UT's Jack S. Blanton Museum of Art (www.blantonmuseum.org).

Both Micheners died in the 1990s, she in 1994 and he in 1997. They are buried in Austin Memorial Park, but the famous author is honored with a marker in the Texas State Cemetery as well.

Michener, James:

He came to Texas to write a book and stayed.

you know you're in
texas when...
. . . the cook can shoot

You've got to ask how he got his name, right? Doris. For a boy. In Texas. That could be downright unhealthy.

The story is that Doris Miller was named by the midwife who assisted with his birth in Waco in 1919. Before the birth she felt sure that the baby would be a girl. Fortunately for him, he was soon tagged with the nickname Dorie.

He grew to be a strapping boy and played fullback on his high school football team. Less than a month before his 20th birthday, he enlisted in the United States Navy. Eventually Miller was assigned to the USS *West Virginia* as a mess attendant; he also became the ship's heavyweight boxing champion.

At Pearl Harbor on the morning of December 7, 1941, he was collecting laundry when he heard the alarm sound for general quarters. In the midst of the Japanese attack on his and other anchored ships in the harbor, Miller was assigned to carry wounded sailors to places of greater safety.

His task completed, Miller raced to an unattended deck gun. As a black man, he had never been trained to shoot it—but shoot he did, saying later that he thought he hit one of the Japanese planes. For his valor he was awarded the Navy Cross, per-

Miller, Dorie:

A boy named Doris has to be tough, and this one was. His bravery during World War II is documented in the movie *Pearl Harbor.*

sonally presented to him by Admiral Chester A. Nimitz, a fellow Texan. Miller was the first African American to receive the Navy Cross.

Almost two years later, Miller was serving aboard an escort carrier that was torpedoed and sunk in the Pacific Ocean. He was listed as missing and presumed dead. In 1973 the USS *Miller,* a Navy frigate, was named in his honor.

The indigenous people in Texas whom Spanish missionaries hoped to convert and settle weren't easily won over, for the most part. But you've got to give the Spaniards points for trying.

They established their first mission in Texas in 1632 near present-day San Angelo, but there's nothing left of it. Only a small commemorative monument marks the spot historians think might have been the location. The same can be said for many of the 35 other missions that came along in spurts in the 17th and 18th centuries. Yet a few structures remain and are well worth seeing.

The oldest surviving structure of the Spanish missions and related military presidios is in Goliad. The Presidio La Bahía Chapel (www.presidiolabahia.org), built in 1749, is less than a mile from Espíritu Santo (La Bahía) Mission within Goliad State Park. The chapel is still used for regular services.

El Paso has three mission churches still in operation. The largest on El Paso's Mission Trail, which runs south of the city, is San Elizario Chapel, dating back to 1877. (The current buildings are more recent than their 1680 foundations.) The other two are Ysleta Mission and Socorro Mission. For more information, call (915) 534–0677 or visit www.missiontrail.com.

Probably the most famous Texas missions are in San Antonio. Chief among them is

Missions:

Although Goliad has the oldest surviving intact mission structure, El Paso and San Antonio have more famous mission trails.

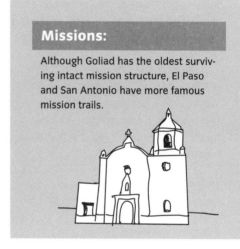

that shrine of Texas independence, the Alamo, but there are four others on San Antonio's Mission Trail on the south side of the city. Together these five provide the most extensive concentration of mission architecture in the United States.

Stop first at the San Jose Mission, where the visitor center for the entire San Antonio Missions National Historical Park is located. Then see Concepción Mission, the oldest structure in the park to have survived without major restoration.

San Juan Capistrano and San Francisco de la Espada Missions are near dams and acequias (ditches) and an aqueduct that make up a Spanish-built irrigation system still in use. For more information about the historic park, visit www.nps.gov/saan/.

you know you're in
texas when...
...you're surfing on sand

If you long for those days you spent in the sand pile, you might want to visit Monahans Sandhills State Park west of Odessa. But be advised that it's a whole lot bigger than the sandbox in your backyard.

The park features almost 4,000 acres of sand dunes, some of which are up to 70 feet high. The vastness of its desert landscape has led some to call it the "Sahara of the Southwest." Actually, the park is only part of an even vaster area that stretches 200 miles up into New Mexico.

Many of the dunes are still active—that is, they continue to grow and change shapes as the wind sculpts them. Others are more or less stabilized by a "forest" of shin oak. The trees hardly seem like a forest since they are seldom more than 3 feet tall at maturity. Yet they may send down roots as far as 90 feet.

For those visitors beyond the pail-and-shovel stage of playing in the sand, the park rents out sand sleds and saucers for surfing the big dunes. The park also has facilities for camping, hiking, and picnicking, and there is a museum and visitor/interpretive center.

Interpretive exhibits show that humans were in the area as long as 12,000 years ago. Later, various Native American tribes used the area for temporary campgrounds and a meeting place. They found game and, amazingly, abundant fresh water beneath the sands. There were acorns from the shin oak and beans from mesquite trees as well.

More than 400 years ago, Spanish explorers were the first Europeans to report seeing the huge hills of sand. For later pioneer travelers and wagon trains, the dunes became formidable obstacles.

Now they attract fun-loving travelers to the state park, which has existed since 1957. For more information, call (800) 792–1112 or visit www.tpwd.state.tx.us.

Monahans Sandhills State Park:

Sliding down a monster sand dune is Texas tobogganing.

you know you're in
texas when...
...you can't wait to see the Neiman's Christmas catalog

Neiman Marcus started out as a family-run organization, but it's never been one of your little mom-and-pop businesses. It was a brother and sister, Herbert Marcus and Carrie Marcus Neiman, and Carrie's husband, Al, who founded the specialty store in 1907. And they were thinking high-end merchandise and customer service from the start.

The Dallas store soon developed a reputation for high prices as well as high quality. Some disparaging consumers called it "Needless Mark-ups." But the store continued to grow and prosper. Its wealthier clientele included oil-rich landowners and those from the cotton aristocracy.

Stanley Marcus, Herbert's oldest son, joined the business in 1926 and became its driving force. One of his innovative retailing ideas was a bit of a spoof on the upscale—and maybe uppity—image of his store. In 1960 he and his brother Edward created the now legendary "his and hers" gifts as the centerpiece of the annual Christmas catalog.

Suggested for the man or woman who has everything, the outrageous gift offerings have included submarines, hot-air balloons, Egyptian mummy cases, and a private concert by Sir Elton John. Most are priced in the millions, but for the more budget-minded, there is always a fancy car priced at a mere $65,000 or so.

Neiman Marcus:

Begun as a specialty store in Dallas, this Texas institution now has an international reputation.

Even Neiman's cookie recipes are expensive if you believe a persistent urban myth. According to the legend, a patron requested the recipe for the store's popular chocolate chip cookie and received both the recipe and a bill for a substantial amount of money. Neiman Marcus has contradicted that story by simply putting the recipe on its Web site with an invitation to print it out and send it along to friends.

Although still headquartered in Dallas, Neiman's now has 35 stores across the country, and a Marcus is no longer at the helm. Nevertheless, the company still claims to adhere to Herbert Marcus's tenet: "It's never a good sale for Neiman Marcus unless it's a good buy for the customer." Keep that in mind the next time you're shopping for an Egyptian mummy case.

you know you're in
texas when...
... you're boot scootin' to a Willie tune

Perhaps no Texas singer/songwriter has left a more indelible mark on the American musical landscape than Willie Nelson.

Born in a small Texas Hill Country town in 1933, he says his upbringing there had a real influence on his formative years as a musician: "I was raised and worked in the cotton fields around Abbott with a lot of African Americans and a lot of Mexican Americans, and we listened to their music all the time. I guess that's why I was influenced a lot by those around me—there was a lot of singing that went on in the cotton fields."

His only music education beyond that absorption of musical styles came from mail-order courses provided by his grandparents and from listening to big bands, Texas-style country, and Frank Sinatra. Maybe that's why it's still hard to pigeonhole Nelson's music. In the 1970s it came to be called "outlaw" country because it had hints of rock 'n' roll, jazz, western swing, and folk and did not conform to Nashville standards.

When you get right down to it, Nelson doesn't conform much to anybody's standards. He looks more like an old hippie than a country star. He wears his hair long and sometimes braided, dresses in T-shirts and blue jeans, and ties a bandanna around his neck or head.

Nelson's recorded albums include more than a dozen that reached number one on the *Billboard* Top Country Albums chart. One of his best-known singles, "On the Road Again," seems to sum up his touring philosophy: "The life I love is makin' music with my friends / And I can't wait to get on the road again."

Also known for his philanthropy, Nelson is generous with his time and talent; he performs for benefits and produces his own annual Farm Aid and Fourth of July concerts.

In 1998 Nelson received Kennedy Center Honors, and a star-studded television special honored his 70th birthday in 2003. Often asked these days when he plans to retire, he always gives the same answer: "All I do is play music and golf—which one do you want me to give up?"

Nelson, Willie:

This outlaw country singer/songwriter returned to Texas from Nashville to become an American legend.

you know you're in
texas when...
...you're a news junky

A Texas journalist made such a name for himself as a national broadcaster that his own name became synonymous with the position of news anchor. Swedish anchors are called Kronkiters; in Holland they are Cronkiters.

Walter Cronkite, although born in Missouri, grew up in Houston and studied journalism at the University of Texas at Austin. He worked in several Texas cities early in his career before gaining national attention as a correspondent during World War II.

Cronkite joined CBS in 1950 and began anchoring the CBS Evening News in 1962. His unflappable demeanor earned him the nickname "Old Ironpants." His honesty and objectivity earned him the title "the most trusted man in America."

Initially only 15 minutes long, the Evening News expanded to 30 minutes in 1963. Cronkite's first 30-minute newscast included an exclusive interview with President John F. Kennedy. Just two months later, Cronkite was the first on the air to report Kennedy's assassination in Dallas. And "Old Ironpants" wept.

When Cronkite retired from the Evening News in 1981, he signed off with his trademark "And that's the way it is." He was succeeded by another Texan, Dan Rather, a native of Wharton.

Rather had already helped make the CBS Sunday night news program 60 Minutes the highest rated, and he continued working on a second edition of the show. He also hosted another CBS news show, 48 Hours—all the while holding down the top job in American broadcast journalism on the Evening News. As a result, he earned his own reputation as "the hardest working man in broadcast journalism."

Rather stepped down in 2005 after 24 years as anchor, although he, like Cronkite, has continued his journalistic activities.

News Anchors:

For more than 40 years—from 1962 to 2005—a Texan anchored the CBS Evening News.

Texas seems to attract feisty, independent women, so it's not surprising that Elisabet Ney settled and worked in the Lone Star State.

Born in Germany in 1833, she was a saucy one there, too. She declared early on that she did not intend to live "the sweet, uneventful life of a German hausfrau" like her mother. Instead, the young Elisabet announced that she would become a sculptor, a more artistic version of her father, a stonecutter. And she did.

At 19 she went on a hunger strike until her parents relented and allowed her to study at the Munich Academy of Art (she was the first woman to study sculpture there) and then work with one of Europe's finest sculptors in Berlin.

In 1871 Ney and her husband, Edmund Montgomery, came to Texas, fleeing political intrigue in Europe. Right away she began to raise eyebrows, even on the frontier, by wearing a black Prince Albert's frock coat, white britches, and knee-high boots and by riding astride her horse rather than side saddle. Furthermore, she kept her own last name and referred to her husband as "my friend, Mr. Montgomery."

Whatever folks may have thought of her unfeminine behavior, there was never any question about Ney's skill as an artist. In 1891 she was commissioned to create stat-

Ney, Elisabet:

A cutter in more ways than one, she lived out the role of the eccentric artist.

ues of Sam Houston and Stephen F. Austin for the 1893 Chicago World's Fair. She went to work even before her new studio in Austin was completed, but only Houston's sculpture made its way to Chicago. She didn't finish Austin's in time.

Both statues are now on display in the state capitol building in Austin, along with the one Ney created of Confederate general Albert Sidney Johnston. When early critics pointed out that Austin's statue was considerably shorter than Houston's, Ney said that the likenesses were as faithful as she could make them and that "any dissatisfaction should be taken up with God."

Today Ney's Austin studio, a structural cross between a Greek temple and a German castle, is the Elisabet Ney Museum. Call (512) 458–2255 for more information.

69

you know you're in
texas when...
...a local boy rules the high seas

Chester Nimitz was an unlikely candidate to be an admiral in the Navy. He was born in the landlocked, predominantly German community of Fredericksburg in central Texas. As a boy he really wanted to go to West Point but settled for Annapolis.

Perhaps he was destined for the sea from the start. His grandfather, after all, built a hotel in Fredericksburg shaped like a steamship. And until he was six, young Chester and his mother lived and worked in the hotel. At any rate, Nimitz made the most of his opportunity for an education at Annapolis and finished seventh in his class of 114. Somewhere along the way he became a Navy man through and through.

His first command was nevertheless a bit of a disaster. Of course, he was only 22, but he managed to run his ship aground on a mud bank and received a court-martial for "hazarding" a ship of the U.S. Navy.

He more than redeemed himself during the rest of his career, ultimately commanding all U.S. and Allied military forces in the central Pacific theater during World War II. During this time he made all the right moves, particularly during the Battle of Midway, still considered the greatest victory of the U.S. Navy.

Nimitz was one of only four men promoted to the grade of fleet admiral during World

Nimitz, Chester A.:

Born in a small landlocked town in central Texas, he went on to command 5,000 ships during World War II.

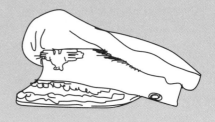

War II. When Japan surrendered, he was the one who signed the surrender document on behalf of the United States. His devotion to the Navy, by this time, was so great that he turned down numerous business opportunities promising much higher salaries. Nimitz was the last surviving five-star admiral when he died at age 81 in 1966.

His grandfather's Steamship Hotel in Fredericksburg has been restored and now houses the National Museum of the Pacific War, formerly called the Admiral Nimitz Museum and Historical Center. For more information, call (830) 997–4379 or visit www.nimitz-museum.org.

you know you're in
texas when...
...you can't find water for all the oil

Probably everyone who moves to Texas dreams of striking oil in the backyard. Some of the natives may, too. Bringing in a gusher is an unlikely event these days, but Texas certainly has had its share of oil booms.

Of course, Native Americans knew about ground-level oil seeps for centuries before anyone figured out much use for the black stuff. They used it to treat a variety of ailments. The Spaniards later used it to waterproof their boots.

Right after the Civil War enough people were using oil products for lighting and lubrication that purposeful drilling took place near the east Texas town of Nacogdoches. Later in the 1800s came the first big producing oil field at Corsicana.

That oil was discovered, however, by accident as local businessmen were drilling for water, not oil. In fact, the first drillers in the area were so annoyed at finding oil zones that they often drilled past them to get to the water they were seeking.

So it wasn't until 1901 that the first true boom came from the Spindletop gusher of Anthony Lucas near Beaumont. Defying the odds and the skeptics, Lucas had kept on drilling in the salt dome formations on Spindletop Hill until a geyser of oil erupted from a depth of more than 1,100 feet. It blew a stream of oil 100 feet high for nine days until it was finally capped and flowed at an estimated 100,000 barrels a day. At that point, that one well was producing more oil than all other wells in the United States combined.

It helped usher in the liquid fuel age that brought forth the automobile, the airplane, the highway network, improved railroad and marine transportation, the era of mass production, and our dependence on oil.

Texas still produces more oil and gas than any other state. Indeed, if it were a nation, it would rank as one of the top 10 producers, according to the Railroad Commission of Texas, which has jurisdiction over oil and gas production.

For information about the Spindletop–Gladys City Boomtown Museum in Beaumont, see www.spindletop.org.

Oil Wells:

Though not as thick as they once were on Spindletop Hill, they're still producing.

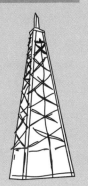

you know you're in
texas when...
... you're fascinated by the notorious

Texans seem to celebrate their outlaws—at least the dead ones. Romantic Robin Hood–like legends have grown up, for example, about the likes of train and bank robber Sam Bass, killed in a shootout in Round Rock in 1878. Now there's a street named after him that ironically runs past Round Rock Cemetery, where Bass is buried. Souvenir hunters chipped away pieces of his original tombstone, so a new granite marker has replaced it.

Then there are all the stories about native Texans Bonnie Parker and Clyde Barrow. They became nationally known outlaws before they were ambushed and killed in Louisiana by Texas Rangers in 1934.

Stories of the pair kidnapping lawmen and robbery victims and then releasing them far from home, sometimes with money to help them get back, added to the outlaws' mythic aura. Their celebrity status and glamorous image were further enhanced by the romanticized movie *Bonnie and Clyde* (1967), starring Warren Beatty and Faye Dunaway.

The two outlaws are buried in Dallas but not in the same cemetery. Clyde is in Western Heights Cemetery; Bonnie is in Crown Hill Memorial Park.

One of Texas's deadliest gunslingers was John Wesley Hardin. Despite the fact that he killed more than 40 people, he had a gentle-man's reputation among those who knew him. And Hardin always insisted that he never killed anyone who didn't need killing.

Born in Bonham, the son of a Methodist minister, Hardin studied law while serving time in a Texas prison and established a practice in El Paso in 1895. Although he was apparently going straight, he made threats against an officer who arrested a lady friend. The officer later walked up behind Hardin as Hardin sat in on a dice game and shot him dead.

Hardin is buried in Concordia Cemetery in El Paso. The fenced-in gravesite is included in tours of the city. As far as we know, hardly anyone visits the graves of the lawmen who brought the outlaws down.

Outlaws:

Dead or alive—but mostly dead—many have achieved celebrity status in Texas.

you know you're in
texas when...
...church art happens in small towns

You can't judge a book by its cover. True enough. And you can't always tell what the inside of a country church will look like by viewing its rather plain exterior, either.

At least that's the case with the Painted Churches of Fayette County. Seen from the outside, they appear to be fairly typical frame, brick, or stone structures with a single steeple. But once you step over the threshold, you witness an explosion of color—almost every surface inside is covered with exuberant murals.

Texas has more than 20 painted churches, 15 of which are listed in the National Register of Historic Places. They were a well-kept secret until the late 1980s, when a local priest began conducting tours. Pretty soon the chamber of commerce in Schulenburg saw opportunities to draw some tourist trade and began to publicize the churches' unique art style.

Located in the rolling hills between San Antonio and Houston, Fayette County was settled by German and Czech immigrants beginning in the 1850s. They built churches and decorated them in the Old World manner.

From simple stenciling to elaborate frescoes, the paintings on the walls and ceilings in the churches retain their vibrant colors—including Pepto-Bismol pink in one church. Inscriptions on the walls are writ-

Painted Churches:

Although there are more than 20 of them in Texas, the 4 around Schulenburg get the most attention.

ten in Czech and German. Finely fitted woodwork is faux-finished to give the appearance of stone and polished marble columns.

The names of some of the artists have been lost, but much of the painting was done by itinerant artists who advertised in church bulletins and newspapers. Sometimes the church pastor or community members would wield brushes themselves.

The Schulenburg Chamber of Commerce provides guided tours as well as maps for self-guided tours to four churches in the nearby towns of High Hill, Dubina, Ammannsville, and Praha. Call (979) 743–4514 or visit www.schulenburgchamber .org for more information.

you know you're in
texas when...
...there's a gash in the plains

Humans have been roaming Palo Duro Canyon for approximately 12,000 years. The first were nomadic tribes hunting for mammoth and giant bison. Nowadays they're tourists hunting for a good campsite.

Generally called the "Grand Canyon of Texas," Palo Duro Canyon starts just east of the Panhandle city of Canyon and stretches some 120 miles down to Silverton. It's up to 20 miles wide and 800 feet deep, making it the second-largest canyon in the United States.

Because of the abundant mesquite and juniper trees down in the canyon, early Spanish explorers dubbed the place *palo duro,* or "hard wood." Later inhabitants no doubt named the stream that carved it: the Prairie Dog Town Fork of the Red River.

The Civilian Conservation Corps took on the chore of building roads and a visitor center and other buildings back in the 1930s after the state of Texas purchased the land in the upper canyon. Palo Duro Canyon State Park officially opened on July 4, 1934. The same rustic stone visitor center, which now houses a museum and museum store, still serves at the rim of the canyon.

Palo Duro Canyon:

Among U.S. canyons it is second in size only to the Grand Canyon.

In addition to the usual park activities of camping, hiking, horseback riding, bird watching, and the like, there is the popular outdoor theater production *Texas.* During the summer the musical presents glimpses of early Panhandle culture in the Pioneer Amphitheatre, with sheer canyon walls as a backdrop. For information or tickets, call (806) 655–2181 or visit www.heritageent .com.

To learn more about the park itself, call (806) 488–2180 or visit www.tpwd.state .tx.us.

Even people who never haul anything more than groceries are likely to own a pickup in Texas. In a recent year, one out of every four new vehicles sold in the Lone Star State was a full-size pickup truck—nearly double the national average—making Texas the nation's leader in pickup sales.

Auto manufacturers have noticed. They're prone to give their pickups Texas-friendly names like Ranger and King Ranch. Furthermore, they know that in Texas, bigger's better. So new designs feature bigger engines, bigger tires (sometime duals in the rear), and crew cabs that provide full backseats and four-door convenience.

Every year the Texas Auto Writers' Association gives its Truck of the Year Award, and it's for pickups, not semis. The competition is stiff at TAWA's annual truck rodeo, but the manufacturers come hoping to grab their share of the Texas market.

Pickup ownership seems to be a cultural thing in Texas. There was a time when pickups were humble farm vehicles—the earliest ones were homemade modifications of Model Ts. But somehow they evolved into high-tech preferred rides with leather-covered seats and power everything. Even Texas womenfolk are buying and driving pickups.

Many Texans still work on farms or ranches or in the oil fields, of course, where a pickup might actually be practical and useful. But the bottom line is that, in Texas, driving a pickup is just plumb cool.

It remains to be seen if rising gasoline prices will dampen Texans' enthusiasm, as full-size pickups are definitely not gas savers.

Pickup Trucks:

Texas leads the nation in the sale of these vehicular status symbols.

Of the three U.S. presidents claiming to be from Texas, one really truly was. The other two were born Yankees and just got to Texas as fast as they could.

Lyndon Baines Johnson, the 36th president, was born near Johnson City (named after his family) and had a ranch near Stonewall in central Texas. In his will he donated the LBJ Ranch to the public, stipulating that it must be a working ranch and not "a sterile relic of the past."

Now the Lyndon B. Johnson National Historical Park (www.nps.gov/lyjo), it partners with the Lyndon B. Johnson State Historical Park (www.tpwd.state.tx.us/park/lbj). Johnson died in 1973 and is buried at the ranch.

The Lyndon Baines Johnson Library and Museum (www.lbjlib.utexas.edu) on the University of Texas campus in Austin is the most visited presidential library in the nation. It's also the only one that doesn't charge an entrance fee.

Presidents 41 and 43 are a father and son both born in New England: George Herbert Walker Bush in Massachusetts, George W. (the *W* stands for Walker) in Connecticut.

Bush 41 moved to Texas after graduating from Yale University in 1948. After he left the presidency in 1993, he said he was going home—back to Texas. And he did, settling in Houston, although he still has that summer home in Kennebunkport, Maine.

The George Bush Presidential Library and Museum (www.bushlibrary.tamu.edu) is on the Texas A&M University campus in College Station.

Bush 43 moved with his parents to Texas when he was only two and grew up in Midland and Houston. His childhood home in Midland, restored to the 1950s period during which he lived there, is now open to the public.

At this writing, George W. Bush had not yet named the site for his presidential library, although several universities and cities have submitted proposals. When it's built, the Lone Star State will have the most presidential libraries in the country.

Presidents:

Three U.S. presidents have claimed to be from Texas, but only LBJ was a true native son.

If you've ever been to a rodeo or watched a western movie or television program, then you've see an American quarter horse in action.

Although it began in the Virginia and Carolina colonies as the first breed of horse native to the United States, the American quarter horse made its transition from racing sprinter to cow horse in Texas.

American quarter horse stallions were mated with mustang mares used on the Texas range to produce strong, agile mounts capable of enduring the harsh climate and rugged conditions on the cattle trails. Speed and strength were the principal traits cowboys required in a horse for all their gathering, roping, branding, and other chores on the open range and, later, on ranches.

A legendary racer named Steel Dust was brought to Texas from Kentucky in the 1840s. In a quarter-mile match race with a local favorite in Collin County near McKinney, Steel Dust won the race and earned a reputation for speed. His descendants were prized by cowboys for use on ranches, and he became the most influential sire for the Texas strain of American quarter horse.

It wasn't until 1940 that a group of American quarter horse enthusiasts got together in Fort Worth and formed the American

Quarter Horse:

This breed, first noted as a quarter-mile racer, evolved into a working Texas cow pony on ranches and in arenas.

Quarter Horse Association, now headquartered in Amarillo.

The AQHA maintains pedigrees of 3.7 million registered American quarter horses, making the breed the world's largest. It is also the world's most versatile, as it is now bred for arena events like rodeo and cutting horse contests, as well as for racing and ranching.

Visitors to the American Quarter Horse Heritage Center and Museum in Amarillo are treated to exhibits, video productions, and hands-on displays highlighting the history of the world's most popular breed of horse. For more information, call (806) 376–4811 or visit www.aqha.com.

The King Ranch in south Texas covers 825,000 acres. That's roughly 1,300 square miles, bigger than the state of Rhode Island. And it's not even historically the biggest. At its height, the JA Ranch up in the Panhandle controlled more than a million acres, and the XIT had more than three million acres and covered 10 Panhandle counties.

One of the persistent legends is that the XIT brand stood for "10 in Texas," referring to the number of counties. But most historians agree that one of the ranch's owners was simply looking for a brand that could not be easily altered by rustlers.

The XIT is no more, having been sold off in smaller parcels. But the romance of the place lives on through the annual XIT Reunion and Rodeo in Dalhart. Dalhart also has the XIT Museum (806–244–5390). One of the old ranch division headquarters buildings is in the National Ranching Heritage Center in Lubbock (806–742–0498).

The King Ranch is still a working ranch and remains one of the largest privately owned ranches in the country. It runs 60,000 head of cattle and 300 horses and is recorded on the National Register of Historic Places as the "Birthplace of American Ranching."

The ranch dates back to 1853, when Captain Richard King, a Rio Grande pilot,

Ranches:

In Texas they're so big that they're measured in square miles as well as acres.

camped along Santa Gertrudis Creek and saw the potential for a cattle range. The now-famous Santa Gertrudis strain of beef cattle—the first new strain developed in the Western Hemisphere—later was bred at the ranch.

Pretty much everything in the city of Kingsville relates in one way or another to the King Ranch. In town are the King Ranch Museum (361–595–1881) and the King Ranch Saddle Shop (361–595–5761 or 800–282–5464). Daily guided tours of the ranch itself are available from the King Ranch Visitor Center (361–592–8055; www.king-ranch.com).

you know you're in
texas when...
...poisonous snakes give you fair warning

When a Texan talks about there being a snake in the grass, sometimes he means a real one. The big four venomous snakes that humans should pay attention to in the state are cottonmouths, copperheads, coral snakes, and rattlesnakes.

Texas has some 10 rattlesnake species and subspecies, more than any other state except Arizona. Three of those are most likely to interact significantly with humans: the prairie rattler; the eastern timber or canebrake rattler; and the biggest, baddest one of all, the western diamondback.

The latter's scientific name is *Crotalus atrox,* with *atrox* meaning "frightful" or "grim." Sure enough, it's the rattlesnake most willing to bite, and it can grow to more than 7 feet long. In legend and lore it has become the signature snake of Texas.

Not that anyone wants to be a part of this statistic, but the good news is that annually very few people die from rattlesnake poisoning—less than 1 percent of those bitten. As a matter of fact, herpetologists tell us that bites are rare because, for the most part, the snakes are terrified of people and know they aren't food, so they want nothing to do with them.

That said, people are still advised to use caution and certainly to pay heed if they hear that characteristic warning whir coming from the rapid movement of the dry, bare scales at the end of a rattler's tail.

For more than 50 years, small towns in west Texas have held early spring roundups of this snake that many people love to hate. Begun as attempts to control the abundance of rattlesnakes causing problems for farmers, ranchers, and their families, the roundups have turned into festivals complete with parades and the crowning of Miss Snakecharmer.

Sweetwater, about 40 miles west of Abilene, claims to have the world's largest rattlesnake roundup each year the second weekend in March (www.rattlesnake roundup.com). On average almost 6,000 pounds of rattlesnakes are collected in Sweetwater annually. Conservationists and animal rights activists are generally not happy about it, but the locals say those folks don't have snakes as neighbors.

Rattlesnakes:

Of the 10 or so rattlesnake species in Texas, at least 1 is found in almost every county in the state—not that most people are looking very hard.

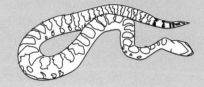

you know you're in
texas when...
...you're feeling independent

Texas was its own country for 9 years, 11 months, and 17 days. It declared its independence from Mexico on March 2, 1836, at Washington-on-the-Brazos. In the revolutionary battles that followed that same year, Texas lost at the Alamo on March 6, had 300 unarmed Texan prisoners massacred at Goliad on March 27, and finally won at San Jacinto on April 21.

Most Texans favored immediate annexation by the United States, but the United States was not all that eager to take on the new nation. Texas was broke, after all, and still threatened with continued war with Mexico. So Texans began doing what they could to establish a stable government and nation. They elected a president, Sam Houston, and decided to declare the city of Houston the national capital.

They continued to fend off Mexican raids on the border and Indian raids on western frontier settlements. In time American sympathy for the Texan cause prompted the U.S. government to approve annexation in 1845. Texas became the 28th state.

Texas was still broke, but it had more land then than it does now. As a break-away republic, it had claimed all of present-day Texas as well as parts of present-day New Mexico, Oklahoma, Kansas, Colorado, and Wyoming. This excess it was willing to cede to the federal government in exchange for the United States' assumption of its debt.

Texas did not surrender any of the public lands within its current boundaries, however, so any federally owned lands in present-day Texas have actually been purchased by the government. Texas also retained the right to divide itself into as many as five states if it ever wants to.

A persistent urban legend says that because Texas was once an independent nation, it can fly its flag at the same height as the U.S. flag. The truth is that *any* state flag may fly at the same height as the U.S. flag as long as the nation's flag is on the state flag's right (viewer's left). Just so you know.

Republic of Texas:

Texas is the only state other than Hawaii that has ever been an independent nation.

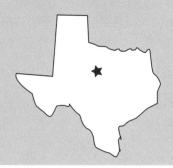

you know you're in
texas when...
...you're counting the seconds

Events are short but exciting in rodeo, the official sport of Texas. Cowboys must ride bucking broncs or bulls for eight seconds and then be judged for style. Ropers, bull-doggers, and barrel racers are competing against the clock and each other for the best time.

Rodeo (the Spanish word for "roundup") can trace its beginnings to the 16th century, when Spanish conquistadors and Spanish-Mexican settlers introduced horses and cattle in the Southwest. That led ultimately to the heyday of cattle ranching and cattle drives in the 19th century.

Vaqueros and cowboys began showing off. They would hold contests to see who was best at bronc riding, team roping, and tie-down roping—chores they did routinely as part of their jobs. Sometimes the competition pitted one ranch's cowhands against another's. Sometimes the cowboys would stage their own contests at the railhead at the end of a cattle drive. These informal events almost always drew a crowd.

Rodeos then moved to town, so to speak. The west Texas town of Pecos claims to be the "home of the world's first rodeo," although there's some dispute about that. Pecos was indeed the scene of a contest in 1883 that had cowboys thundering down Main Street roping steers and corralling them on the courthouse square. It was at least the first to give prizes, apparently.

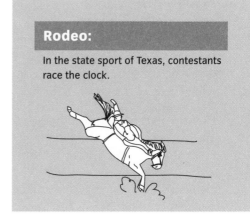

Rodeo:

In the state sport of Texas, contestants race the clock.

But credit Wild West shows in the late 1800s for popularizing rodeos and making them part of show business. Some moved indoors, the first in Fort Worth in 1917.

By the 1920s promoters and cowboys began to organize, standardize the events, and create the sport we know today. The Rodeo Cowboys Association evolved out of an earlier organization oddly named the Cowboys Turtle Association. (One explanation for the name is that the cowboys were slow to unite.) Houston hosted the reorganization meeting in 1945. Now there are organizations for women professional rodeo athletes and for high school and college rodeo competitors.

Among the top seven rodeos in the United States today, in terms of prize money given, are ones held in San Antonio, Houston, and Fort Worth.

you know you're in
texas when...
...you're down by the riverside

The stretch of waterway that is now San Antonio's popular River Walk was almost drained and made into a paved-over storm sewer. But a bunch of concerned women in the San Antonio Conservation Society vigorously opposed the plan.

This same group of women had already battled city officials and engineers who proposed straightening bends in the San Antonio River and taking out several historic buildings in the process. The women invited city commissioners on canoe rides to see the river's scenic beauty along its natural course. They also staged a puppet show titled *The Goose That Lays the Golden Egg*. The commissioners apparently got the moral of the play and agreed to "spare this Goose [the river] for future use." That all happened back in the 1920s.

Thanks to a visionary young architect named Robert H. H. Hugman, the banks of the Paseo del Rio (River Walk) eventually became a world apart, one level below the city's busy streets. Hugman even envisioned gondolas plying the river as if in a Texas version of Venice, Italy.

No gondolas appeared, but there are barges. Rio San Antonio Cruises provides half-hour narrated tours aboard slowly moving boats along the 2.5 miles of the river bend development. Informed guides share historic tidbits and a few laughs

San Antonio River Walk:

This popular entertainment destination—second only to the Alamo in terms of local tourism—thrives in the midst of the city.

along the route. That's the best way to get oriented.

You also may want to walk along the river past the hotels and restaurants and shops. Trees and other plantings provide a park-like setting in an almost tropical landscape, and occasionally strolling musicians entertain.

If you walk at night, however, you may want to carry a flashlight. Although the pathways are lighted and the river is fairly shallow, there are no guardrails. You can fall in. So you may want to limit the number of margaritas, too.

For more history and a guide to events, see http://thesanantonioriverwalk.com.

An unruly army of Texans commanded by Sam Houston managed to overwhelm a superior Mexican army on April 21, 1836. It was the battle that gained Texas its independence from Mexico and its beginning as a republic.

On what is now called the San Jacinto Battleground, a force of 910 Texans took General Antonio López de Santa Anna's troops by surprise in an afternoon attack. According to Houston's report, 630 Mexicans were killed and 730 taken prisoner—all in about 20 minutes. Only 9 of Houston's men were killed and 30 injured.

To commemorate this decisive victory in Texas history, a monument was begun 100 years later as a Public Works Administration project. It was finished in 1939 and is dedicated "to Heroes of the Battle of San Jacinto and all others who contributed to the independence of Texas."

The monument is a 570-foot limestone shaft topped by a 34-foot, 220-ton star symbolizing the Lone Star Republic. The structure is listed in the *Guinness Book of World Records* as the world's tallest stone column memorial (almost 15 feet taller than the Washington Monument in Washington, D.C.).

In its base is the San Jacinto Museum of History, which houses a collection that spans more than 400 years of early Texas history. The museum's bronze doors carry reliefs of the six flags of Texas.

The San Jacinto Battleground State Historic Park is a 1,200-acre site that has been undergoing extensive renovation since 2001. Located within minutes of downtown Houston, its actual address is in La Porte. For more details and directions, call (281) 479–2431 or visit www.sanjacinto-museum.org.

San Jacinto Monument:

The world's tallest war memorial honors those who fought for Texas independence.

you know you're in
texas when...
... you see a half dozen flagpoles

According to one story, Angus G. Wynne Jr. first wanted to name his new theme park Texas Under Six Flags. But his wife said no because "Texas isn't *under* anything." So he and his backers called it Six Flags Over Texas, and the rest is history.

Well, actually the history came first, since the park's name derives from the fact that Texas has been governed under the flags of six different nations: France, Spain, Mexico, the Republic of Texas, the Confederate States of America, and the United States.

Wynne, a wealthy oil man and real estate developer, got the idea for an entertainment park in his home state after visiting the newly opened Disneyland in Anaheim, California. Planning for the Texas project began in 1959, and construction in Arlington commenced the next year. The park opened in August 1961.

Initially, the Six Flags theme determined the focus in each section of the park. The Spain and Mexico section, for example, featured Spanish-themed rides, attractions, and buildings. Nowadays the state-history component is joined by pop culture icons like Batman and Superman and Looney Tunes characters as new attractions continue to be added.

Six Flags Over Texas in Arlington was the first of what is now a chain of venues owned by Six Flags, Inc., the world's largest regional theme park company. It owns and operates a total of 29 parks in North America, serving 34 of the 50 largest metropolitan areas in the United States. Its corporate offices are now in New York and Oklahoma City.

You've got to wonder what Angus Wynne's wife would have to say about that.

For more information about Six Flags Over Texas, call (817) 530–6000 or visit www .sixflags.com/parks/overtexas.

Six Flags Over Texas:

This theme park, which originated in Texas but is now a national chain, takes its name from the state's history of revolving governments.

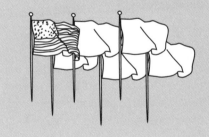

Although Texas might not be everyone's first choice as a beach resort, surely those thousands of spring breakers can't be wrong. Every year come March, they start swarming to South Padre Island.

This small resort community is at the southern tip of a sand-barrier island (the longest barrier island in the world) extending some 110 miles along the coast of south Texas. Only 3 miles across at its widest point, the island nevertheless has the longest sand beach in the United States.

In between the developed tips of Padre Island (Corpus Christi is at the northern end) is one of the last natural seashores in the nation. The Padre Island National Seashore (www.nps.gov/pais) preserves an unblemished 80-mile stretch in the middle.

But that's not where the partying is. For that you cross the causeway from Port Isabel to reach South Padre Island. The Laguna Madre is in between, and the Gulf of Mexico is on the other side of the island.

Unless you're a college student bent on having a good time with a whole bunch of other college students, however, you may want to avoid South Padre Island in early spring. Come earlier or later to try some water sports, deep-sea fishing, shelling, horseback riding, boating, sand castle building, or dolphin or bird watching.

South Padre Island:

At the southern end of the longest (mostly) undeveloped barrier island in the world, this beach resort is a party destination for thousands of college students every spring.

Or you can just hang out on the beach or go to one of the many restaurants that serve fresh seafood harvested daily from the Gulf. The partying is optional.

For more good ideas, contact the South Padre Island Visitors Center at (956) 761–6433 or (800) 767–2373 or visit www.sopadre.com.

Some Texans may have way too much time on their hands, so they build things like the Stonehenge. Yep, if you can't make it to the Salisbury Plain in England to see the real one, you can do the next best thing and see a slightly larger than half-size replica close to Hunt in the Texas Hill Country.

Conceived by Al Shepperd and Doug Hill and built by Hill, the new version of the monument started with a single slab of limestone. Hill, a tile contractor and builder, had the stone left over after building himself a patio. He offered it to his neighbor, Shepperd.

Shepperd had it set upright in a field on his property but decided he needed more. Hill and Shepperd built a 13-foot-tall arch behind the stone to accentuate it, and, well, one thing led to another.

Pretty soon the two men were reinventing Stonehenge in the sense that they put it back together again rather than leaving it partially toppled like the original. Aside from that one slab of limestone, however, the rest of the creation is fabricated from steel, metal lathe, and plaster anchored in cement.

A year and a half after Stonehenge II was completed, Shepperd added a couple of *moai*, 13-feet-tall heads, like those on Easter Island, further confounding our sense of geography. He was talking about adding a

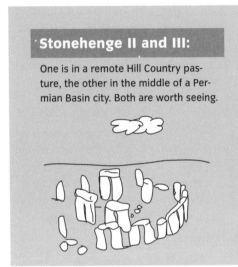

Stonehenge II and III:

One is in a remote Hill Country pasture, the other in the middle of a Permian Basin city. Both are worth seeing.

replica of an Alaskan totem pole, but his death in 1994 put an end to his collection.

Shepperd's family still owns the property and provides free access to the site, if you can find it. Take Highway 39 out of Ingram to Hunt and then Farm Road 1340 to the meadow on the south side of the road. As you come around a curve in the farm road, there it is—a surprise even when you're looking for it. Visit www.alfredshepperd .com/stonehenge/main.html for more information and a map.

But wait. There's yet another Texas Stonehenge, completed in 2004, on the University of Texas of the Permian Basin campus in Odessa (www.odessacvb.com/historical_ sites.html). Take your pick.

you know you're in
texas when...
...you're likely to hear a whopper

Texans take great pride in their ability to lie. They have contests to see who's the best liar, and they host concerts to show off those who can best pull a leg and stretch the truth.

Houston holds a liars' contest each year, appropriately sometime around April Fool's Day, in which the winner is promised a "solid gold trophy." Austin's contest is in February. Of course, Austin liars claim that the competition is especially stiff in the state capital, given that the legislature meets there.

In 2005 Becky Allen, director of the George West Storyfest, proposed a statewide contest. "No one else was doing it," she said, "so we are." She has even copyrighted the Texas Liar's Contest name. Now liars gather annually in front of the courthouse in this town of fewer than 3,000 residents to have a lie-off.

The contest is part of the annual story-telling festival in George West the first Saturday in November. See www.georgewest storyfest.org for details.

The Texas Storytelling Festival (www.tejas storytelling.com) features some of the state's best liars each spring. And the Texas Folklife Festival (www.texancultures .utsa.edu) has a special liars' concert during its summer run each June.

Tall tales are certainly nothing new in a state with a reputation for exaggeration. Cowboys told whoppers around the campfire and created a model for the likes of folk hero Pecos Bill. Hunters and fishermen have long been making colorful claims about the ones that got away.

Note that early on, men were the principal liars. What seems to have changed is that lying is now an equal opportunity activity: More women are competing—and winning. And that's no lie.

Tall Tales:

Liars in Texas have contests to see who's best.

Once upon a time . . .

Even before Texas became a republic and later a state, it had a navy. That was the first, formed by the provisional government when hostilities broke out between Texas and Mexico. It amounted to four schooners purchased in January 1836.

During the Texas Revolution the navy's primary charge was to protect lines of supply between New Orleans and Texas. The harbor at Galveston served as home port.

The first Texas Navy lasted until mid-1837, by which time all four ships had been lost. Two were captured or destroyed by the Mexicans, one was lost in a storm, and one was sold because the impoverished Texas government couldn't pay the repair bill.

So there was virtually no Texas Navy between September 1837 and March 1839, when the first ship of the second navy was commissioned. Six more ships were added, once again to guard against sea attacks from Mexico and to protect shipping lanes.

What ships remained of that fleet were transferred to the U.S. Navy in 1846, shortly after Texas was annexed as a state in 1845. That could have been the end of the Texas Navy story. But in 1958 Governor Price Daniel established the third Texas Navy, and Governor Preston Smith reestablished its original base in Galveston in 1970. Largely commemorative, of course, this navy exists primarily to ensure the survival of Texas naval history.

The current navy is the strongest of the three, ironically. Her flagship is the battleship *Texas,* now berthed near the San Jacinto Monument in La Porte. Other World War II vessels adopted into the third Texas Navy include a couple of PT boats and a submarine in Galveston; the aircraft carrier USS *Lexington,* moored at Corpus Christi; and a destroyer built in and now returned to Orange to serve as a museum.

The oldest ship in the Texas Navy is the *Elissa,* a tall sailing ship built in 1877. She is now part of the Texas Seaport Museum in Galveston. Still seaworthy, the *Elissa* sometimes sails away, so check locally for the dockside schedule. Call (409) 763–1877 or visit www.tsm-elissa.org.

Texas Navy:

Count 'em: Texas has had three navies since the days of the Republic. It is the only state to have had even one.

you know you're in
texas when...
...you'll take 'em lone or in a company

"A fiery horse with the speed of light, a cloud of dust, and a hearty 'Hi-yo, Silver!'" With those words radio listeners, and later television viewers, were invited to "return with us now to those thrilling days of yesteryear. The Lone Ranger rides again!" The adventures of a sole surviving Texas Ranger and his faithful Indian companion, Tonto, led them to "fight for law and order in the early West" through many episodes.

This fictional hero with his mask and silver bullets helped add to the mystique of a unique group of law enforcement officers. More recently we have *Walker, Texas Ranger,* to keep them spotlighted in popular culture. But their real history is pretty interesting all by itself.

More or less authorized into being by impresario Stephen F. Austin in 1823, the first Texas Rangers were formed as two companies of men "to act as rangers for the common defense" while Texas was still under Mexican rule. Their main charge then was to protect early settlers from attacks by hostile tribes.

During the run-up to the Texas Revolution, the Rangers became much more official, and their numbers increased to three companies of 56 men each. The Gonzales Ranging Company of Mounted Volunteers was the only group to answer Colonel William Barrett Travis's call for assistance in defending the Alamo against Santa Anna

Texas Rangers:

Since the 1820s they've fought the bad guys off and on the screen.

and his Mexican troops; the volunteers died alongside the other defenders in the historic battle there.

From the beginning of the Republic in 1836 to statehood in 1845, the Rangers were the primary defense for Texas. Their mission, until well after the Civil War, was to guard against Indian and Mexican incursions. As the 19th century came to a close, however, their responsibilities changed from military protection to law enforcement, duties they continue to perform today as part of the Texas Department of Public Safety.

The Texas Ranger Hall of Fame and Museum in Waco displays Ranger memorabilia and Ranger-related popular culture artifacts. For more information, call (254) 750–8631 or visit www.texasranger.org.

Temple Houston, Sam's son, got pretty flowery with his language when he accepted the new capitol building on behalf of the people of Texas in 1888. "Texas stands peerless among the mighty," he said, "and her brow is crowned with bewildering magnificence! This building fires the heart and excites reflection in the minds of all."

Well, at least it's turned out to be a big tourist attraction in Austin, the capital city.

The current capitol building is actually the third. The first was built of plank lumber, and the second—a Greek Revival structure—burned in late 1881. That same year an architect named Elijah. E. Myers won a nationwide design competition for the project.

He proposed a square tower with a mansard roof. Nope, the Texans said, we want a cast-iron dome like the one on the national capitol. Myers proposed native limestone or sandstone for the exterior of the building, but the limestone streaked when exposed to air.

So Myers suggested Texas pink granite, also a native stone. It would be more expensive, but your average Texan is a fair horse trader. Owners of a granite quarry near Marble Falls agreed to donate the stone in exchange for a rail connection to Austin. The Austin and Northwest Railroad

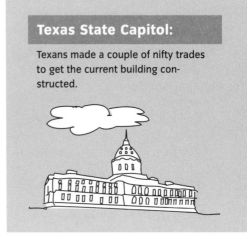

Texas State Capitol:

Texans made a couple of nifty trades to get the current building constructed.

built an extension to carry the granite to the building site.

The trading wasn't over. In exchange for constructing the capitol, contractors were offered three million acres of land in the Texas Panhandle. This acreage would become the famous XIT Ranch.

The capitol opened to the public on San Jacinto Day, April 21, 1888. The largest state capitol building in the United States, it is second in size only to the national capitol. Its dome is almost 15 feet higher than its Washington counterpart.

For more information, visit the State Preservation Board online at www.tspb.state.tx.us.

you know you're in
texas when...
...you understand that *y'all* can be singular

Technically speaking, *y'all* is already a plural, meaning "you all." But Texans also use it to call out individuals, preferring *all y'all* when they really want to get the attention of a whole group.

Texans think other people talk funny. Meanwhile, foreigners—that is, those who live in other states—sometimes need a translator to explain what a Texan means when he says, "I'm fixin' to go over yonder a fur piece and mosey around for a spell."

Texans can be all swole up, all choked up, or all worked up about something and determined to carry on come hell or high water. They'll 'fess up to being fit to be tied and sometimes to throwing a hissy fit.

A Texan can be a maverick (wild, independent loner), a galoot (rascal), or an old cuss (bad-tempered rascal).

Even a Texan's insults can be colorful: You can be ugly as a mud fence, dumber than dirt, all hat and no cattle, crooked as a dog's hind leg, older than two trees, or tighter than bark on a tree. You can look as if you've been rode hard and put up wet.

On the other hand, you can be cute as a possum, tough as a boot, big enough to hunt bear (make that "bar") with a switch, and you'll do to go to the well with.

Then there's that Texas twang and the dialectical habit of reducing two words or two syllable sounds to one: "you all" to "y'all," as a classic example, or "fire" to "fahr." Technically, the result is a monothong, which has nothing to do with skimpy one-piece garments.

A good many grown men in Texas are still called Bubba, a baby-talk version of "brother." These days the moniker has taken on redneck connotations and is used as a generic group noun as well as a name, as in "I saw a bunch of bubbas down at the truck stop this morning."

At least Texans are slow talkers, which makes it easier to pick up on their peculiarities of speech. So y'all come to see us now, you hear?

Texas Talk:

It doesn't take a Henry Higgins to pick a Texan out of the crowd just by listening.

You're all hat and no cattle!

When people ask, "Just what is Tex-Mex, exactly?" Texans generally start naming some of the major Tex-Mex food groups: nachos, enchiladas, chili, crispy tacos, fajitas, margaritas. But the hybrid word *Tex-Mex* started out designating the Texas version of pretty much everything Mexican.

That's what the *Oxford English Dictionary* says anyway. The *OED* also says that the word didn't appear in print in relation to food until 1973. And it was first used, generally, in a derogatory way to suggest that Americanized versions of Mexican food were vastly inferior to the original cuisine found in Mexico's interior.

Disdain from food snobs has never bothered Texans very much, however, and they went on enjoying what they had always called Mexican food. It was the rest of the world that initially took up the new label as Tex-Mex restaurants sprang up in Paris and other European cities and even spread to Asia and South America.

Pioneer providers of Tex-Mex, before it even had a name in its home state or anywhere else, were pushcart vendors. They sold chili and tamales and pecan pralines in the streets of Texas cities during the last couple of decades in the 19th century.

In the first half of the 20th century came the old-fashioned Mexican restaurants that nevertheless catered to Anglo tastes. They usu-ally featured a variety of combination plates with a mix of enchiladas and tacos and refried beans. If you looked in the kitchen, you were likely to see a big can of lard. The food was fairly bland by today's standards.

In the 1970s the new term (*Tex-Mex*) emerged, along with a new taste: hotter and spicier. As Americans became more health conscious, they also became wary of those lard-laden combination plates. They began to expect flour tortillas, fresh salsas, and grilled meat seasoned with chili peppers.

Today the label *Tex-Mex* is no longer an insult. For a more comprehensive history of the word and the cooking style, see *The Tex-Mex Cookbook: A History in Recipes and Photos,* by Texas author Robb Walsh.

Tex-Mex:

Applied to foods, this label describes a unique cuisine that has evolved from Texas versions of Mexican cooking.

The Sons of the Pioneers sang it in the 1940s: "See them tumbling down / Pledging their love to the ground / Lonely but free I'll be found / Drifting along with the tumbling tumbleweeds."

The tumbleweed, also called a Russian thistle or wind witch, does go drifting along like a rolling skeleton across prairies and highways in west Texas and in the Panhandle. And as it goes, it disperses seeds—as many as 250,000 per plant.

Some may be surprised to learn that the tumbleweed is not native to Texas. It came from the arid steppes of the Ural Mountains in Russia. Speculation is that it made its way to the United States around 1877, probably transported in some flaxseed imported by Ukrainian farmers in South Dakota. Within two decades it had tumbled into a dozen states, including Texas.

The young plants send up bright green, grasslike succulent shoots, usually striped with red or purple. Mice, bighorn sheep, and pronghorn antelope feed on them in the wild. During severe droughts farmers have even tried using young tumbleweeds for hay and silage.

But it's the mature, dried thistle everyone recognizes. Sometimes a whole line of them will be caught in barbed wire fences as if mounted for display. They may be as

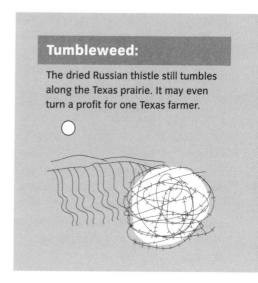

Tumbleweed:

The dried Russian thistle still tumbles along the Texas prairie. It may even turn a profit for one Texas farmer.

small as a soccer ball or as large as a compact car.

Invasive weed that it is, the tumbleweed nevertheless amuses the young, who chase it, toss it, and herd it into massive collections. It has been the focus of craft projects and decorated like a Christmas tree.

So maybe it was inevitable that someone would try raising tumbleweeds as a cash crop. That's the case on the Texas Tumbleweed Farm in Petersburg, near Lubbock. You can order small, medium, large, or Texas-size weeds, but the shipping may cost you more than the product itself. How do you pack one of those things, anyway?

Texas has its share of tree huggers, to be sure, but it also has had at least one turtle hugger. Ila Fox Loetscher died in 2000 at age 95. Everyone on South Padre Island called her the Turtle Lady.

Her fame spread beyond the island. In the early 1980s she appeared on the *Tonight Show* with Johnny Carson and brought one of her sea turtles wearing a dress and panties. At the risk of being called eccentric (or worse), she dressed her turtles up, she said, to get the attention of those she wanted to teach about the turtles' plight. Her legacy lives on.

In 1977 she founded Sea Turtle, Inc., initially to assist in the protection of the endangered Kemp's Ridley sea turtle. The scope of the organization has expanded to support the conservation of all species of marine turtles.

Principal threats to the turtles include exploitation of eggs and meat at the nesting beaches (this was especially the case during the 1960s) and incidental drowning from fishing operations in the Gulf of Mexico (turtles get caught in nets and on lines). The animals also fall prey to the effects of pollution.

Although the days of dressing turtles and having them do tricks (Loetscher figured out that by "tickling" a turtle under its flip-

The Turtle Lady:

Gone but not forgotten, this South Padre Island resident played dress-up with endangered turtles to get the public's attention.

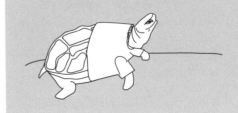

per pit, she could get it to wave good-bye) are over, volunteers still hold demonstrations at Sea Turtle, Inc., on South Padre.

Call (956) 761–4511 for a current schedule of shows and viewing hours, or visit www.seaturtleinc.com. Oh, and there really is a turtle hotline. If you're on the beach and see an endangered sea turtle, call (956) 380–9677.

The Rose Capital of America is nestled in the piney woods of east Texas. That would be Tyler, home of the nation's largest municipal rose garden.

It all came about because of a peach blight, more or less. From its beginnings in the 19th century, Tyler and the rest of Smith County relied on agriculture as the mainstay of its economy. At first cotton was the leading cash crop, but then truck farming and fruit orchards became increasingly important.

By the turn of the 20th century, there were more than a million fruit trees, mainly peach, in the county. But along came a peach blight that wiped out much of the fruit industry. A good many farmers then turned to growing roses.

You see, the climate and rich soil around Tyler are ideally suited for growing roses, and by the 1920s the rose industry had developed into a major business. By the 1940s more than half the supply of rose bushes in the United States was grown within 10 miles of Tyler.

Naturally, this success led to a festival, still celebrated in Tyler every fall. The Texas Rose Festival attracts 100,000 visitors or so each October, when the Tyler Municipal Rose Garden is in full bloom.

The garden is actually a 14-acre park planted with almost 40,000 rose bushes of at least 500 varieties. Sizes vary from the miniature roses no bigger than a dime to the large blooms on tall grafted rose trees. You may want to bring a pad and pencil to write down the names of your favorites.

Other activities include what Texans expect at any festival: a parade, a show, the crowning of a queen, and the serving of refreshments—although the Queen's Tea is a far cry from beer and barbecue. Visitors can also tour the Tyler Rose Museum, which highlights the history of the local rose industry and the rose festival. For more information, call (903) 597–3130 or visit www.texasrosefestival.com.

Tyler Roses:

These beauties are displayed in the nation's largest rose garden and celebrated with a festival each fall.

It's been said that Texas has four seasons: drought, flood, blizzard, and twister. Someone else once described Texas weather as long periods of drought interrupted by floods. And there's more truth than exaggeration to those observations.

By its sheer size Texas is likely to have all kinds of weather—some of it all at once. Summers can get hotter than a two-dollar pistol and winters colder than a well digger's knee. Cold weather comes as northers or blue northers, depending on the intensity of the storm, and a hard rain can be a gully washer or a frog strangler.

Statewide temperature records range from a low of −23 degrees Fahrenheit to a high of 120. The deepest snowfall from a single storm measured 33 inches, and the highest sustained winds in the state were clocked at 145 miles per hour, with gusts up to 180 miles per hour. The wettest year across the entire state produced 42.62 inches of rain, the driest only 14.30 inches.

More tornadoes, or twisters, have been recorded in Texas than in any other state, again partly due to its size. An average of 132 tornadoes touch down here each year. The greatest Texas tornado outbreak on record was spawned by Hurricane Beulah in 1967—115 tornadoes in a five-day period. Texas had a total of 232 tornadoes in 1967, the most in a single year.

Speaking of hurricanes, Texas has those, too. One of the greatest natural disasters ever to strike the state occurred on September 8, 1900, when a hurricane devastated Galveston, killing 6,000 people. Since hurricanes began getting names, the Texas coast has been hit by the likes of Audrey, Carla, Cindy, Celia, Allen, Danielle, Alicia, Bonnie, Claudette, Ivan, and Rita, to name a few.

Folks along the coast know to board up the windows and evacuate when a storm is coming, and those on the plains hightail it to the storm cellar. In between weather events they pray for rain or take out more flood insurance. It's a way of life.

Weather Extremes:

Texans deal with the heat and cold, the wet and dry, the windy and calm—sometimes all in the same day.

Texans, by and large, are a friendly lot. The name of the state, after all, is derived from the Hasinais word for "friends or allies" or "friendship." The native tribes of east Texas used the term *thecas* or *tayshas* more as a greeting, apparently, than as a group name. And the early European explorers and settlers were no doubt glad to hear what they translated as a congenial "Hello, friend."

When it came time to decide on a state motto, the 45th Texas Legislature picked the word *Friendship* in 1930. Today state motorists are reminded by highway signs to "Drive friendly."

Some take that urging to heart, especially in the Panhandle and in far west Texas. They wave to other drivers they meet on the roads and highways. But it isn't a full-handed wave; it's true economy of motion. The waver generally has both hands on the steering wheel, one hand at the 11:00 position, the other at 1:00. As another car and driver approach, the waver, still gripping the steering wheel, lifts only the index finger of his dominant hand.

That's it, although the gesture may be accompanied by a moment of eye contact and a slight nod of the head. Oh, sometimes—if there has been a recent rain and the crops look good—the occasional

West Texas Wave:

Especially on rural Texas roads, you'll see it: one index finger raised in greeting.

driver, in his exuberance, may lift two fingers. But that's rare.

You know you're really settling in as a Texan when you start waving back.

you know you're in
texas when...
... the bluebonnets come back

The state flower of Texas could have been the cotton boll or the cactus bloom. Those were two of the proposals when the state legislature finally got around to choosing an official blossom in 1901.

Never mind that the cotton boll is not really a flower. One legislator spoke emotionally in favor of it because cotton was king back in those days. Another fellow argued for the cactus so eloquently that he earned the nickname "Cactus Jack." That was John Nance Garner, later vice president of the United States under FDR.

But it was the National Society of Colonial Dames in America that won the day with their choice: *Lupinus subcarnosis,* "generally known as buffalo clover or bluebonnet," according to the House resolution. There was more squabbling later, however, as it turns out there are five varieties of bluebonnet in Texas. Furthermore, the most prolific and popular is actually *Lupinus texensis,* which blankets central Texas every spring.

The Bluebonnet Wars raged off and on for 70 years until the legislature finally added *Lupinus texensis* "and any other variety of bluebonnet not heretofore recorded" to the official state flower listing. So technically, Texas has five state flowers (so far).

Spring is certainly a prime time to visit Texas, as that is when the most wildflowers are in bloom. Far west Texas has its yellow

Wildflowers:

Lady Bird Johnson's home state plants thousands of them each year to help "beautify America."

poppies spread on the foothills of the Franklin Mountains. Central and south Texas put on the most colorful show of all with an abundant mix of bluebonnets, Indian paintbrush, Indian blanket, and coreopsis.

The Texas Department of Transportation helps Mother Nature along by planting 33,000 pounds of wildflower seeds along the state's roads and highways each year. Each pound includes about 170,000 seeds and at least 30 varieties. TxDOT even provides a wildflower hotline to advise visitors about peak times and the best viewing places (800–452–9292).

Then there's the Lady Bird Johnson Wildflower Center in Austin (512–292–4200). Native plants bloom there year-round, but the center is especially colorful in spring.

Waylon Jennings got it right, declaring in one of his songs that "Once you're down in Texas, Bob Wills is still the King." The King of Western Swing—that's how Wills is usually tagged. Not that he invented the genre, but he certainly popularized it beginning in the 1930s.

It was in the unlikely little Texas town of Turkey that a mix of country, cowboy, jazz, and blues took hold of a young fiddler. He began a musical odyssey that ended only with his death in 1975. He played first with his father, also a fiddler, at farm dances in rural Texas.

Then he put together his own groups and added instruments unconventional in western bands: drums, brass, steel guitars. He finally formed Bob Wills and His Texas Playboys. Sometimes he had more musicians in the Playboys than there were in the so-called big bands of the era.

And he talked. Right in the middle of a song Willis would call out, "Take it away, Leon." And electric steel guitar player Leon McAuliffe would play a solo riff much as a jazz musician might. Or Wills would simply utter his signature high-pitched "Ahh ha!" as if to punctuate a special spot in the music.

Although Wills made more than 500 recordings, two songs are best remembered, and he wrote both of them. "San Antonio Rose" grew out of an instrumental piece he first titled "Spanish Two-Step." And the words to "Faded Love" came long after his father had fiddled out the tune.

The influence of Wills is most notable these days in the style of Asleep at the Wheel. In fact, their motto is "Western Swing ain't dead; it's just Asleep at the Wheel." George Strait also has covered a number of old Wills tunes.

Wills was elected to the Country Music Hall of Fame in 1968. The town of Turkey celebrates its native son at the annual Bob Wills Reunion in April and at the Bob Wills Museum (Sixth and Lyle Streets). The museum houses fiddles, boots, hats, recordings, music, and photos. And you can still hear the occasional "Ahh ha!"

Wills, Bob:

He grew up on a farm just north of Turkey and went on to become the King of Western Swing.

you know you're in
texas when...
... the snowbirds light and hitch

They make their great escape from snow shoveling every winter and head south into Texas. Generically, they're called snowbirds, but in south Texas, where they roost in the greatest concentrations, they're called Winter Texans.

Mostly it's Midwesterners who flock to Texas to flee the frozen north. They light in RV parks and senior-oriented communities in the Rio Grande Valley especially. Winter Texan season runs from November to April.

The mild climate is the biggest draw, of course, but there are lots of activities planned for these guests to keep them happy and pouring money into the state's economy. According to a recent biannual study by the University of Texas–Pan American, more than 140,000 Winter Texans directly infused $329 million in one year into the Valley's economy.

The UT–Pan Am survey concluded that the average Winter Texan couple is from the Midwest, stays about three and a half months in the Valley (usually in a recreational vehicle or mobile home) and spends about $4,700 during the visit.

Some of the largest RV resorts in the world are in places like Harlingen, Mercedes, and San Benito. With well over 1,000 spaces each, they can accommodate a lot of motor homes, fifth-wheels, and camping trailers. Built around golf courses, tennis courts, and swimming pools, these destinations offer country-club-like atmospheres you don't find at your average KOA.

So the Winter Texans keep coming back year after year, and some of them decide to just stay. And why not? How much fun can it be to sit by the pool, sipping a margarita in the dead of winter, and call your snow-shoveling friends up north to ask, "Guess what I'm doing?"

Winter Texans:

That's what snowbirds are called in the Lone Star State.

you know you're in
texas when...
... "the Babe" does not mean Ruth

Mildred Ella Didriksen's father, Ole, was a seafaring storyteller. Her mother had been an accomplished skater back in Norway. They came to Texas and lived in Port Arthur, where Mildred was born.

After the 1915 hurricane they moved to nearby Beaumont, where Ole, who was also a carpenter, built a gymnasium in the backyard. Little Mildred grew up to be an athlete. And a storyteller.

First of all, she took the name "Babe," claiming that the boys on the sandlot called her that because she could hit home runs like Babe Ruth. She could, by all accounts, but some say that her mother gave her the nickname.

Babe also changed the spelling of her last name to Didrikson, emphasizing that she was Norwegian, not Swedish. She cared about her image. She even fibbed about her age, saying she was born in 1914 instead of 1911, as her baptismal records indicated.

But one thing she had no need to exaggerate was her ability on virtually any playing field. Her high school basketball team never lost a game if she was playing. She single-handedly won an Amateur Athletic Union championship track meet by scoring 30 points. The second-place finisher, with 22 team members, scored only 22.

By virtue of her wins in that meet, she qualified for five events in the 1932

Zaharias, Babe Didrikson:

Arguably the best athlete of the 20th century, she did it all.

Olympics. The rules allowed women to compete in only three back then. She won two gold medals and one silver (and that only because she went over the high jump bar head first, a foul in those days).

Didrikson discovered golf and met George Zaharias in the 1930s. She married George and began winning tournaments, more than 80 in all. She was the first American to win the British Women's Amateur Championship and the first woman to work as a resident professional at a golf club.

The Associated Press named her Woman Athlete of the Half Century in 1950. She died of cancer in 1956 and is buried in Beaumont, where the Babe Didrikson Zaharias Museum is located (409–833–4622 or 800–392–4401).

index

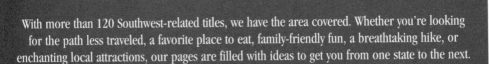